Great Poets Across America

A Celebration of National Poetry Month

Brooke Alexander
EDITOR

Washington, D.C.

Great Poets Across America:
A Celebration of National Poetry Month (II)

Library of Congress
Cataloging in Publication Data

ISBN 978-1-61936-050-1

Printed and manufactured in the United States of America by

Foreword

For the past sixteen years, poets and poetry have been celebrated every April during National Poetry Month. The Academy of American Poets as well as schools and literary organizations all over the country dedicate this special time to increasing appreciation for poetry in American life and assuring its perpetuality.

As most of you will agree, poetry enriches our everyday life in many ways. It puts us in tune with our surroundings, the environment, current events, and, of course, our own thoughts and feelings. It encourages reflection—something most of us do not take enough time for in today's busy world—and, most importantly, sharing. And this is what National Poetry Month is all about: sharing your time, your poetry, and your artistic visions with others as we work together to spread awareness of poetry across America.

In honor of our poetic heritage, we have compiled this volume of verse to represent today's ever-growing community of amateur poets. Each of you can proudly say you made an active contribution to National Poetry Month 2012, and one that will be read and shared by many. We hope throughout the year you continue to find new, innovative ways to share poetry with others and to encourage others to get involved. Poetry's relevancy in modern culture is attibuted to the written legacy of our American poet forefathers. Today, we must keep this art alive and thriving!

Brooke Alexander
Chief Editor

In Our Short Forever Together

I want to conquer a clock with you,
Shatter the face and hang on the clicks as they clank.
Hide behind a roman numeral or two.

I want to plunge off the hour holding your hand,
Feel your palm sweat in mine as we stand up to the
Minute Men.
I'll capture your second in an instant.

I want to face Father Time with you at my side,
Hold on as his ever-growing fingernails that help him
count the hours reach out for us.
Immortality has made him spiteful.

I want to tick your tock,
Feel the bell toll resonate from your core as we embrace.
Leave me at midnight.

Deborah Cerwonka

Aerial View

Sometimes I dream that I can fly
Searching treasures on the earth
I ponder the beauty of this world
As each tiny cell gives birth...

When you're in pain I'll fly to you
And pick you up to hover with me
The air's so crisp and woods so lush
We'll sip straight from the stream

Our song of life as angels sing
With harmony in the tune
We'll dip and soar and touch our wings
Then bathe in a lagoon...

When sun is set we'll fly back home
And settle in the nest
All night we'll cuddle and cozy up
Our life is just the best!

With morning sun it's up again
To view things from above
We'll look at everything so different
When all we see is love...

Wanda Jeanne Beardslee

Wanda Jeanne Beardslee is a sixty-six-year old mother of three and loving grandmother of six beautiful grandchildren. She worked for many years as a legal secretary. She worked in the law office of former Governor of Tennessee, Frank Clement. She also was the second employee hired at Opryland Hotel and worked through the design, construction and operational phases of the incredible Gaylord Opryland. In 1980 Wanda bought a Merle Norman franchise and owned and operated two franchises for thirteen years as a sole proprietor. When she sold her last studio, she had 5,000 women in her card file whom she calls friends. For twelve years Wanda worked as a realtor and she is a Life Member of the Million Dollar Club. Wanda is happily married and deeply in love with her husband Dennis Beardslee, a Wilson County builder. Wanda has been writing poetry since she was a teenager and has been published in newspapers, periodicals and anthologies. She has lived in and around Nashville, TN for fifty years.

Silence and Shadow

From silence and from shadow
my singing spirit came,
putting behind the soundless reaches,
quitting, at last, the darkened chambers,
seeking the pure unsullied beauty
of color's never-known reflection,
of music's still unheard melodic.

With daring and with courage
this mortal round began,
trying the new untried endeavor,
besting the heretofore unconquered,
answering for all time the challenge
of an eternity of error,
of life's universal emptiness.

For passion and for pleasure
the jeweled time was spent,
testing the new-awakened senses,
feeding the flame of frank desire,
trading the wealth of years of wisdom
for joys no more remembered,
for loves no longer loved.

To duty and to honor
the molten soul was forged,
conquering at last passion's pleasure,
taming the strength of daring courage,
coming at last through fiery trial
to ambition's full surrender,
to agony's final murmur,
to silence and to shadow.

Larry Johnson

Another Piece of My Heart

Drifting like a leaf right-out-of-the-blue.
A deep and truly honest, "How are you?"
I mean to say, "I'm fine," but I can't speak.
I'm trying to be strong, but tears are not weak.

The tatters of my heart are all still inside.
I look and I listen, and yet they hide.
My voice breaks the spell and trumps my best.
The crashing of the waves is pulling my chest.

Oops, I found another piece of my heart.
Suddenly, now, the tears start.
A lump in my throat, reaching for sound,
I'll mend it to the others in the lost-and-found.
Maybe, this time, it will start to seem round.
I found another piece of my heart.

Pierced by mercy,
The beauty of love,
The power of duty,
And faith restored breaks my bounds

And found another piece of my heart.
Suddenly, now, the tears start.
They keep rolling down, shaking my ground.
I owe it to the others in the lost and found.
Maybe, this time, it will start to seem round.
I found another piece of my heart.

Glen Cooper

"Another Piece of My Heart" was intended to be a song. The first two stanzas are the verses. Stanza three is the first chorus. The fourth stanza is the bridge. Lines three and four of the fifth stanza are the only changes to the first chorus for the second chorus. Line one of the fifth stanza is the only change to the first chorus for the final chorus.

The Sculptor

Visualizes a familiar face
unaware of what he's sculpting
choosing the perfect stone of
just the right hue
as he looks
from the abyss of marble
he wonders what onlookers
are thinking about his
detailed appearance

Joshua Kramer

Time Distant, but Here

A burnt down city, broken remnants remain.
I count severed heads to keep from going insane.
Abandoned, alone, cast away from the rest.
I need duct tape to keep my heart in my chest.
Observing the sky I see it's raining ashes.
I'm scared, won't anybody. Somebody!
Please help me before my life crashes.
Skinless corpses leave a bloody trail.
Brainwashed zombies, my will will prevail.
Drooling brutes stand in front of a TV
Wave my hands in the air, but they can't even see me.
Entire nations fall prey to their phones.
Countless generations, they all seem like drones.
Walking the streets of a city once was.
Too much to take in, I...I have to just pause.
I burst into flames and fly towards the sun.
The end of our race has more than already begun.
Since the beginning we've fought one another.
Instead of standing hand in hand showing love to our brothers.
Hate has clouded judgement, rage flows through our minds,
Liars, stabbing backstabbers, and scum of every kind.
Human evolution? I don't know. Have we really?
Becoming even worse, the bottom of the barrel
To all incoming citizens, WARNING: Enter at your own peril.
Still there are some whose love burns brighter that Sirius
The one and only Dog Star, yes I'm being serious. Not at all delirious.
When it comes to choosing sides, why's your mind so tedious.
Pure or evil, hurry up choose wisely.
Just be sure the path you choose doesn't lead to your demise, see?

Cristan Juarez-Secundino

Gambler's Prayer "I'm All In"

In the game of chance babe
When odds are stacked so high
I tip my hand to you babe
Pray for two of a kind

My chips are on the table
My breath I hold so tight
The jackpot is a big one
The gamble is in sight

I'm all in
You are my royal flush
I'm all in
To no one else I trust
I'm all in
We gamble now as one

Let's spend our life together
Prove the dealer wrong
Play our last hand ever
The King of Hearts I've won

In the game of chance babe
When odds are stacked so high
My signal goes to you babe
The aces are all mine

Nadine Dockstader

The Fight Between Good and Evil

In the darkest hours of my life
You were never there for me
I walked these lonely streets
Feeling the depression
As I look at the trials that will never leave me
The dark angel appears
Tempting me with many ways to ease the pain
He asks which will be your choice?
I look at him and say none of them
My choice is for you to leave me alone
Dropping to my knees wishing for something different
Behind closed eyes I see a bright white light
A voice tells me to open my eyes
An angel in white stands before me
Take my hand and open your heart to me
All this pain will be no more
I will be by your side for as long as you want
And in passing I promise streets of gold and no more pain
As I did as he asked my life changed
No more pain and sadness
Seeing things in a different light
If only all could feel what I feel
It is so amazing

Gary Hatcher

The Foolish

Can you be a fool for love,
Just to have it torn from your very arms.

Can you be a fool for having hope,
Only to find that it utterly fails.

Can you be a fool for thinking there is cure,
To find that there never was or can be.

Can you be a fool for not having love, hope, or thought.
For the sake of the sixteen-month-old boy who died in your sister's arms.

Tell me, am I fool for all that?

Marylynn Ryder

Music Isn't Just an Art

Music can control your emotions and actions.
Music can control your feelings and thinking.
The very nip of your mind, can go ultimately blind, by the
rapturing wasting time.
It's the product of a rotating tone, that makes contact
with our bones, and causes the movement of tapping toes.
The blankets of the noted, roam over the water filled with
boats, that numbs the tongue's jokes.
The warmth overcrowds the dry courts, and the tormenting
voices become silenced.
It races through your veins, through small slits.
It flows up to the fingertips, then lays upon your innocent lips.
Don't try and escape it.
It's expanding into the depths of your hurt to kill it, so
your thoughts don't become madly stupid.
Close your eyes and see your world, don't you see it's
magnificently pearled.
Can't you taste the sweat on your hand, and the cool breeze
touching your face.
You get the urge to start running fast paced, and feel the
river sprinkle water upon your tired ankles.
You stop to hear someone giggle and run toward you and you embrace them.
You wish with all of your being that this song will never end.
You feel like you met them before, they smile and say, "I'm sorry, but you
have to go back to the real shore (world).
Our time is limited and almost finished."
You don't want them to leave, they made you feel at ease.
"It's time," says them with a smile that is so beguiled.
There, they disappear from your mind, and imagination.
You open your eyes in tears of frustration, and realize it was a dream.
A dream that made you feel clean and healed your fragile heart.
That is how "music isn't just a art."

Rhemarine Davis-Smith

Music is loved by all people. Music was created to comfort and inspire us. Some people think music is just music, not realizing the impact music has on themselves and others. Depending on the kind of music you listen to, music can be innocent or harmful. My poem explores the power music can have on our emotions, give us a vision or help us to relax.

Relapse

One last relapse,
That will destroy her forever.
It takes away her strength,
And all of her hope too.
It's taking over her life,
There's nothing left to do.
She sits on the floor,
She's holding her wrist.
She knows that if you find out,
You'll be really pissed.
She holds out her hand,
She's reaching out to you.
She's grasping the blade,
She needs to let go.
Show her the way,
Before things escalate out of control.
Her face is hidden within her sleeve,
You look her in the eyes,
And say "You can trust me."
With your help she rises
Up from the floor.
She hands over her blade;
She doesn't need it anymore.

Alyssa Farruggia

Prayer of Peace

If Martin Luther King had a dream
That one day blacks and whites
Would live together in equality
Then I have a dream
That one day
Peace and love
Will reign supreme
Over hatred and fear.
I have a dream of a world
Where children do not have to fear
What lies around them
And where pain comes only
From accidental intentions
As opposed from intent to harm.
And so I pray to
Whoever may be listening
That one day
My dream will come true

Jennifer Melissa Ponce Lara

Peace, I find, is something that we as a species struggle with. This has frustrated me ever since I was a child, but from that frustration came this poem. If everyone could channel their frustration, pain, and sorrow into beauty and creation then I truly believe that we could achieve peace. Until then, however, I simply hope that my poem will reach out to others and help them find peace.

Living Doesn't Mean You're Alive

This is your life, get a grip on it
It's a video game and you have the controllers
Live in the now, decisions don't make themselves
Change is made by action and choice
Choose wisely what you do with your life
We only live once, cease the moment
Relish creativity and dance when no one else is moving
Open your eyes, do you see what I see?
Take my hand and I'll lead you to the path
Where once you go it's hard to come back to other people's reality
Remember, how you perceive things it's just your perception
Cut the puppet strings!
Don't let time get you down
Eternity is just a God's blink away
Smile, just do what makes you happy
Smoke if it makes you happy
Laugh if it keeps you from crying
Every second is valuable, treat it like it counts
Happiness is the key to life, stand up for what is just
Throw your hand in the air, because I'm on this level
I don't even care I just want to be free no matter what
Face your goals face your fears
We have only one opportunity
This is it!

Samantha Estock

Learn universal love, smile and don't take anything for granted, you're here for a reason. Make positive impacts on others. Don't forget this is your life! My inspiration comes from my fellow epileptics like Edgar Allen Poe, Van Gough, Socrates, Joan of Arc, Charles Dickens, Leonardo de Vinci, Chanda Gunn, Thomas Edison, and Harriet Tubman. Without my seizure disorder I would not be who I am today. Thank you universe and God.

A Little Fancy

little dogs
with little tails
on little asses

—tick, tick tick—

little manicured nails
tickling the sidewalks

fancy ladies
showing fancy tail
with their fancy asses—

crimson vivid porcelain claws
clicking one against the other
useless
predatory
rich

winter leaves scatter
bones of a fading skeleton

random tosses
fits and starts

'till, last gasp
they succumb beneath a shower
of perfume and piss

Rev. Rebecca Guile Hudson

To me, writing poems is like painting pictures with words, creating visuals to surprise the mind. I can find poetic inspiration in just about anything, and feel so blessed to have this gift. Except, for me, I don't think of it so much as a gift, but rather as the color of my petals. A flower does not choose what color it is going to blossom into, it just blossoms; I do not choose to write, the writing blossoms through me and I feel very often that I'm simply taking dictation. And I just LOVE that colorful sensation!

You

You made me laugh
You made me cry, that I cannot deny
My heart for you, that you can keep
love, and cherish it, in your sleep
My care for you as strong as the sun
forever you are my love
Don't break my heart it's just for you,
you made me cry oh great
Now, I see you every day chilling alone with
your new babe
Now you guys walk along, hand in hand
Song by song. I know inside were meant to
be, I gave you love, but you rejected me
We were once a love song, sang by us to,
man I keep crying what's wrong with you.
Okay today I saw you hurt she broke your
heart, just in two
I'm sorry about your mistake, I tried to
warn you—
You wanted someone better than me, she
broke your heart, like you did to me.
I wish I could make you all better, just
so you could see how much you
meant to me.

Milia Garcia

Not Just a Dog

Destine to be someone's pet, I am,
and for how long, time will tell.

If I am for the pleasure of some child,
then we can grow together as pals that
would be grand.

If I am to be a show of beauty and be
treated as royalty, it will be a pleasure.

If I am to be an elderly companion, it
will be an adventure of dreams in
someone else's mind that is fine.

If I am to be a guardian in someone's
backyard, as long as I have shelter and a
meal is okay with me.

If I am to be abused and mistreated, I'd
rather die before I am to be born.

There are many reasons for why I am a
dog, it is for your pleasure, to keep you
safe, to keep you healthy, but most of all,
to be your best friend.

Juan Zayas

My writings are moments of inspiration, a desire to let my soul soar and reach out. To brake the silence of the mind and let the heart feel. I am a dreamer. I spent many years in the armed forces and held many types of jobs. I come from a large family of fourteen kids and I am the oldest. I just wish that the world would be a better place before I die.

Saved

When I awaken the dark clouds of
Grief gather across my mind
Threatening a torrent of tears
My heart is squeezed with
Pain
My soul is aching from my
Loss
A piece of who I am has gone
Missing…forever!
Utter emptiness, fiery anger, numbness, deepest sorrow
This is my life now
Loneliness and isolation surround me
Understanding from people I love
Again the dark clouds gather
A message, a voice answering the
Distress call of my heart and soul
Kind words of understanding and support
Flood my being
A ray of light breaks through the clouds
A beam of hope touches my heart and it
Blossoms
Love, understanding, support, friendship
Compassion that runs deep and still
Calm the raging storm of grief
Temper it…
Peace rolls across my soul
An intense sigh of relief, release
Comfort knowing that I am not alone in my agony
Never will I be alone again
The dark clouds may gather again but…
I know the intensity of the storm will wane
I have a shelter now built with
Hope, understanding, support, compassion, friendship and
Love

Michelle Fry

Silence

Silence
Deadly or paradise?
It fills the air
Leaving too much curiosity in the room
The haven it provides
Can be denied
As people are left
Wondering
Silence
The mystical powers it implores
As one by one
Everything goes quiet
Nothing is left behind
Except for
Silence

Mary Rhodes

Sweet Silence

I remember the silence that settles on the forest after sunset,
across the prairie after a soft spring rain,
beside rustic rivers at dawn when deer go to drink,
along the length of a frozen lake glistening in the moonlight,
on still dark downtown streets before the sleeping city stirs,
in empty sanctuaries after all the worshippers have left,
and, in sun-baked gardens so hot that even the birds are still.

I also remember the silence that envelops two lovers
who speak only with their eyes,
holding hands across a restaurant table
or later, after the last deep, satisfied sigh following love-making.
Sweet silence, how comforting it is
to be wrapped together in such sublime stillness
until a gentle awakening at dawn to the haunting coo of a mourning dove.

W. F. "Bill" Cento

We all have a teacher to thank in our lives. Mine is Brother Robert Ernst, S.M., at St. Mary's High School, St. Louis, MO some sixty plus years ago. An English teacher, he encouraged me to write. And write I did, working on newspapers long enough ago to remember the beginning of NATO, the French Indochina War and the death of Stalin. After retirement in 1990, I resumed writing both prose and poetry, but mostly poetry. In the decade of 2000, I was driven by my wife's dementia, my caregiving, her death and my journey to recover from grief. Playing equally important roles were the three women in my life—my mother, Gussie; my wife, Vera Ann; and my companion later in life, Muriel. Now, at eighty, my life flickers like "a candle in the wind." The intimate times with your life's partner are precious to remember, so savor them and rejoice in the memory of the love you shared with the spouse who has slipped away and left you alone.

Reality

Enemies,
So many enemies,

All closing in on me,
All coming from different sides,
All trying to destroy me…
All of them
M

Fighting, kicking, screaming,
To be free of them,
Freedom

Escaping to a black hole…
Nothingness, sweet, sweet,
Nothingness

'Till they come for me again,
When I will awake
Unto a new night of…
Reality

Elizabeth S. Peters

The Ultimate Moment

after light faded
life had retired
air was quiet
waiting for inter rup tion

band of thieves we stole the night
suspension   in time   was over
falling back from our performance
jumping off
            the stage and leaving it behind

night was sliced
warm rain
lights BOOMED on
illuminating night

beyond our halo was (nothing)
but time for   escape that was over
we celebrated its existence
water
falling
from
sky

a disk was   thrown
whipped the breeze
you threw it hard
nearly killed me

we ran in nice, neat cloths
not caring that silk was soaked
not caring that feet were muddy
grass might ruin the knees

because it was over.
so now we took it
took everything back
to keep for the year

we laughed
        and we ran
                and we jumped
didn't speak of the moment we knew it was
last moment before a soul walks   away
before he lets peace slip from his hands

buttimegoesfast
before you know
we're running over warm, drenched football fields again
enjoying a moment for just what it is
a perfect memory hanging out of   reach
of life's desperate greedy claws

Alex Helme

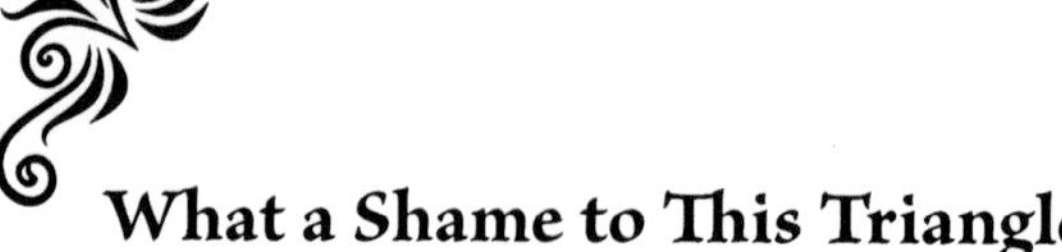

What a Shame to This Triangle

The sheep are wandering, wandering like the early man
Grubbing for a means of survival
Yearning for shelter to protect them
From the sun, the rain and the predators.

Oh! This journey in the wilderness,
The journey of uncertainty
Because of suffering and confusion,
The sheep no longer know the shepherds.

Wandering, wandering in the wilderness,
No oasis like elsewhere in the jungle, they wondered and wondered
Aloud, what is wrong here in the cradle of their fathers?

The journey persists with no shelters
To shelter themselves from the horrors of the wilderness.
Some of the sheep find the journey's end
Discouraging and littered with graves,

The shepherds abandoned for
Greener pastures, Geneva fields
Dream and smile, could they not
Take their sheep along?
No! Bring back the sheep cry.

The sheep cry aloud but no future
For the offspring, no greener grass
In the cameroes. Oh! Shepherds grow for posterity.

Ernest Timnge

I, Earnest Timnge, born on May 28, 1975 at Fundongkom Cameroon was born into a polygamous family of eight wives and with over forty-five children is the last of four children of my mother who was the sixth wife of my father. In the country-side in which I grew up, formal education was of extremely low priority. Parents mostly owing to poverty and ignorant of the value of this type of education hardly sent their children to school. They preferred us becoming local farmers and hunting of game than going to school. After completing primary school in the village, I was fortunate to have been picked up by an uncle, Prof. Nelson Ngoh, who is today teaching graduate students at the University of Bridgeport, Connecticut to live with his family in Yaounde-Cameroon. It was thanks to Dr. Ngoh Nelson that I obtained higher education in Cameroon earning a bachelor of arts degree in Africa-America literature at Yaounde University. I am currently undergoing a masters of education here at Strayer University DC USA.

Broken Mirror

Broken mirror on the wall,
Will you watch me as I fall?

Will you see me
If I break?
Do you know
If I'll ever wake?

Will you watch
As teardrops streak?
Will this mountain
Ever peak?

I try to move on,
but hope is gone.

Broken mirror
can you see,
what will be
the outcome
for me?

Jamie Campbell

Lost Hero

You used to be with me every day,
now you are barely here.
You were my hero
until you were forced to leave
and go somewhere far away.
You battled with alcohol and possible guilt
and lost that battle.
I now live with less loving words from you
and a lost hero.
You were a father with great strength
and my greatest hero.
Now I lost that hero
and gained a changed father.
I will always love and remember
what you were like before.
I will love you with all of your flaws
and cherish the memory of my lost hero.

Kara S. Olson

Untitled

Leave me to die here
breathe deep and cry not
no one's listening
The misery, the pain overtakes me

You left a hole
where my heart should be
Look past the smiles
and the laughs

buried deep inside
a broken heart shattered
and left to bleed

Rain clouds come to play
as she cries herself to sleep
She's tired, beaten and broken

Leave me to die here
I'll ask you to help me survive
here
as you give the last scar
you'll leave me to die here

Brooke Newbold

How Can...?

No clouds in the sky,
Moment slip away,
No friends to hold on to—
Watching you walking away.
How can the moon say
It doesn't need the sun?
How can...?
How can you say
I'm not your type
And in your eyes you try
To hide the truth?
Your love flows in my heart
Like a spring,
Your smile keeps
My soul alive.
How can...you refuse
To let me in your life?
Together we will love like dove,
Our love will rise above
And shine more than a diamond.
Let me take away your fear
And fill your heart with joy.
Darling, my love, I can be any kind
Of man you want me to be.
When everybody disappears I will be
The one to keep you strong.

Vilsoir Satine

Shirley Ann Haley

Sixty-two years ago
A halo glowed
Over the head of a little girl
Who had one curl

Oh how happy her mother was
To see her because
Not sure if she would grow
Or if at all so

This little girl was Shirley
Whose life was enduring
She gave so much to everyone
Now God called her home to serve from above

Although she will be missed
She loved to kiss
All the little ones she met
Even if they are wet

Judy Ann Howe

A Cry of Happy

Within my head
balmy breezes blow
Icy blues begin to melt
Cold winter rules
no longer in my soul
Gone now the sadness
that I've felt.

Beneath frozen feet
snow turns to slush
My toes tingle with the flush
of a warming flow...
I feel mind and spirit
start to glow!

Spring has arrived
without and within me
Caused a flutter in my heart
A tremble in arthritic knees
A buzzing in my head
Like a swarm of dizzy bumblebees

My melancholy fog
is clearing
I find that I'm
no longer blue
Oh blissful joy
as sheer euphoria ensues
A teardrop leaks then
from my eye
Trickles down my cheek
and I wonder...why?
Could it be my state of happiness

deserves itself a "happy cry"?
Must be...I smile...and softly sigh.

Doris Emmett

I never cease to be amazed by the power of the written word. Poetry can move the mountains of a heavy soul and light the darkness of a saddened heart. It breathes and laughs and cries and sighs. Poetry lives in me and letting it out on paper provides no greater release of joy or sorrow or simple gratitude for the gift of life. Life is poetry and poetry is life.

Little on the Mind

Little on the mind,
Not much to be said,
Yet an unknown weight constantly bears on my brain
Every night as I lay in my bed.

I cannot say where the pressure comes from,
Or why it must choose me,
It seems to be almost comical
How it always manages to be.

I read and I write,
I sing songs through the night,
Yet that oblique being called insomnia
Unwelcome visits in the moonlight.

It never says a word
And even dares you to fall asleep,
Then when you try yet do not succeed,
It laughs ruthlessly at your lost feat.

After hours of pure exhaustion,
It yawns and you take lead.
The clock now reads four thirteen
And it finally turns to leave.

Little on the mind,
Not much to be said,
Yet an unknown weight is finally lifted
Early morning as I lay in my bed.

Mandy Isabella McCool

Mandy Isabella McCool has been writing for as long as she can remember. She had her first poem published at the age of ten and has had several other poems and short stories published since then. She has won many awards for her writings. She is now writing a series of novels while going to college to become a registered nurse. She is twenty years old.

Sunset

As the evening sun goes down for the day,
It pays homage to God in a special way.
It paints the heavens as it bids the earth goodbye,
With colors of pink, blue and purple splashed across the sky.
And as the darkness kisses the earth,
The lake dances and shimmers for all its worth.
And the waves lap against the rocks and ground,
Where the beautiful fish jump and the singing loons can be found.
And the grass and trees sway in the gentle breath of air,
While the moon glows bright and the stars shine everywhere.
This glorious show is given to us by the earth, water, and heavens above,
To remind us of the splendor of God and best of all, His everlasting love.

Diane Hunt

Love Me Forever

Enjoy to wonder and dream
If I should fall into the never
Would you still love me forever
What part of me is broken
that love cannot fix
Even with life cruel tricks
Do you see me, as I see you
or do you see me as broken too?
So I close my eyes. I dream
a wonderful dream, I dream
of you. And I realize, for me
this is forever.

Henry Pruitt

The Long Drive

I don't want to let go of our loving embrace,
We've shared a special time in what is now a special place.
Does my voice give away the pain that I feel inside?
Knowing that I must leave you, my tears can I hide?

The road before me stands ready, but I don't want to go.
It's a long journey that awaits me, this I hope you know.
I'll miss your smiles, your laughter, all your little charms.
Achingly, I'll miss your kisses and holding you in my arms.

Seeing the pain upon your face makes this very hard to bear.
The anguish in your eyes tells me parting's pain is shared.
Now, there's a lump in my throat as I begin to drive away.
The tears begin to flow. Oh, how I wish I could stay.

Mile by mile, town by town, unwantingly I drive,
Until we meet again, on memories newly created I'll survive.
My spirit I leave you, please hold it in your heart,
As dearly as I hold yours in mine whenever we're apart.

Thomas C. Menear

To capture a moment in time is a blessing. To be able to make others feel what I feel or see is very satisfying. I never know when something will spark a creative idea. For those who know me, I usually carry two pens at all times, different colors or styles for editing. I'll write on whatever is available at the time. I don't always get a complete thought, but I don't throw any thoughts away. I am honored that my thoughts are deemed worthy for this compilation.

Price of Freedom

Let's live our lives being more than we are, and that way, when they bury us together, they can write on our gravestones that we forgave ourselves, forgave each other, forgave the world.

It isn't a promise of greatness, or earth-shattering perfection. Just a simple prayer; even if we can't become what they want, we can make them proud anyway by being ourselves, flawed and beautiful.

If we can create a fraction more than we destroy, we can make the world remember who we are by what we were willing to give up for the future, and recreate the meaning of the word 'alive.'

We have been the past, are now the present, and will be the future. Take one step at a time, one foot in front of the other. Don't pause, it'll leave you behind. Don't run, you'll leave yourself behind.

If you let me show you hope, I'll hold you as you stumble and learn to walk again. Hope is many things, but, mainly, creation. So, recreate yourself into the person you were meant to be, alive and free.

The question is the answer. Ask if, and you already have the end of an endless thing. It's a gift, powerful and irreplaceable and permanent, and it rises from the ashes of a broken past.

So go ahead, hit replay, remember the pain, and always savor the beauty. They all walk hand in hand as lovers do, an endless circle that lets us know we're still alive, still breathing.

I don't ask you to understand, I don't ask you for anything but a single second to remember who you are, who you were made to be. Never lose sight of this; it is and forever will be your destiny.

He who can learn to forgive can learn to live, and in learning we teach. Any man who follows in my footsteps may learn to lead another, save one more soul from the darkness of the human condition.

There is no perfection in this place...not yet...so let yourself be as gloriously imperfect as you are. You were made to be you, not some sad, plastic thing, incapable of feeling anything, just simply you.

And if nothing else, remember this as something you can turn to when nothing makes sense. The memory of what was sacrificed for you, the light of the world, given to allow you the freedom of self.

Senja Francis Bundy

Women Like Me

On this day, not of my choosing
I obligingly stand off to the side
Trying to make out the lectures of how my future is to be
The future, that my elders came to decide...

I hear their words
Filialness expected of me
And my head flies to a space
Where I know I will never be free....

As my destiny is embarked
On a journey which I can only tag along
I feel the warmth of salt in my tears
And wonder... "Where did things go wrong?"

To have my future decided
Like a blueprint already mapped out
There are none who believe it can differ from the chosen path
Sadly, I only sigh and join the crowd....

I will never know the tenderness
A true lover shows his wife
I will never know the affection
A true man gives with his life....

It brings me great sorrow
Knowing women like me cannot choose
In love or not... Our way of life
Was destined to be measured and ruled....

I can no longer be my family's child
For I am but a daughter
I cannot follow my ancestral line
Because I am believed unable to uphold our honor....

My mind is embedded to fulfill the dreams of my new family
But my dreams, in my heart, are engraved
It's saddening to know that not only am I on "pause"
But that my wishes will never come close to "play"....

Beek Thao

Pandora

A door
A simple white door
That is all it was
Or
That is all it appeared to be
How was I supposed to know
What treacheries lag behind it,
For
No sign
No warning
Just a simple white door
Yet I was Pandora
With her accursed box
Told not to open it at all costs
But
I did
All I did was
Open the door
Now
The world's gone
Lies dying, for once again
Life's woes have been released, all because
Of
A door
A simple white door
That is all it was.

Morgan Ho

Romeo and Juliet

Two lovers meet in the dead of night,
Both to bask in the pale moon's light.

They caress and they kiss without a single word,
Their ears kept alert for a single step to be heard.

They look into each other's eyes, fighting against the dawn,
Because when the sun rises, both will be gone.

How far can they run, how far can they go
To hide from the feelings that they dare not show?

For if people knew how much they loved a stranger,
Surely the two would be in endless danger.

And so, two lovers meet in the dead of night,
They will show their love and devotion...but just for tonight.

Amanda Roswell

My Own Mirror

I look in the mirror and I see a girl with blonde hair and eyes as dark and empty as a deserted waterfall staring back at me. I look out the window it's raining hard and heavy. I close my eyes and all my memories come rushing back. I no longer touch with my hands, but with my ears. I no longer hear with them, but with my mind. Once I close my eyes I am awoken by a world full of dreams and fields full of happiness and love. The face I once knew… my face… Not the girl people have shifted and crumbled to their satisfaction, but the girl who knew innocence and pure love. But when I open my eyes it's all back running, still standing in the same spot looking out into the heavy rain. Still the girl that has been thrown and shifted my world has vanished…

Mary B. Arleth

Porcelain

Blank faces are staring at me
their glass eyes glazed
I'm frightened, and yet I created them
these dolls and statues.

One day they will be sitting
on a shelf.
Collecting dust in a little girl's room.
Then what will I do,
when the blank faces
no longer stare?

Kaylee Sears

What Is Hope?

Hope is the light that you see through the darkest night
A strength you get that allows you to continue to fight
A determination of never giving up no matter how many days in your life get rough
A driven will to survive that cannot be deprived
Hope is not to die but to live and through Jesus Christ you will always have eternal life
Hope is always believing never doubting that God will always make a way when there is no way
So what is hope? God is hope.

Nakia Brown

If I Should...

If I should lose you
I hope you can understand
the love that was there
it was all yours
from the moment it all began
may my soul forever find your soul
may your smile forever place itself on me
may time wait
stand still
for so much time stands
in between you and I
if I should lose you
know that everything stopped at you
the world became perfect
all at you
so may the stars dance and alter
to a time
where destiny finds
a worthy space
where you and I
can meet again
at a perfect time
in a perfect place.

Rocio Soledad Castillo

Blueprint

For blueprints sketch out inner workings of plans.
A device only the operator will know to de-code and take
into consideration their purpose.
A genetic code that could be insights to our intentions.
A distinctive code written in many forms.
These designs may configure well being.
May map driven creativity of a realistic mind.
For we all have blueprints that began in the early stage of life.
It's the complexity of drawings that mend oneself to
continue sketches of the blueprints we ourselves
maintain to thrive to complete.

Richard V. Cash

Hidden in a Crowd

Hidden in the sunlight
Alone within a crowd
Speaking words to no one
That turns to whispers in the wind.
Every day I go home,
Alone to an empty room
And every day I wake up,
To come to this place best known as Hell.
The teachers don't look twice at me,
And other students only judge.
Hidden in the sunlight
Alone within a crowd
Speaking words to no one
That only seem to fade out.

Kaitlin Gadzinski

Matinee

In the distance, drums are heard
People are running
People are screaming
Today is a good day to fight
Today is a good day to die
The bugle sounds
A roar of thunder
The charge of the light brigade
Arrows fly and people die
But the bullets pull us under
The curtain drops
It's the end of the show
Well, Daddy, we almost won that one
Yes, Son, now finish your ice cream
It's time to go....

Keith Gates

I'm Keith Gates, an R.N., currently a case worker for a local hospice organization. I graduated with a bachelor's degree in fine art in 1974 from Santa Barbara Art Institute. American Indians are my main subject matter for my artwork as well as for my poetry.

Hope Beyond the Storm

Look up above, the sky is moving
Clouds are clearing and moving on
Lives are torn and dreams are scattered,
And the journey ahead seems long

But through the tears, hope is all around you
A picture in a broken frame shines through,
Think about that moment, a memory
That can never be taken away from you

Gather round the tattered flag left standing,
Beneath a new sun shining bright
A ray of hope shines down upon you
In the darkness there is always light

Stand up tall and say a prayer
Hold on tight to faith within
Band together and help each other
Rebuild the dreams and start to mend

Hold your head up, reach down deep
For the strength you have inside
Hold the hands of those around you
Look through the dark and find the light

Lacey Rose Simpson Williams

He Called Me Beautiful

We met under a mistake;
Nothing is a mistake about our love.
No matter how weird I can be;
You still choose to love me.
I'm not telling you it's going to be easy;
I'm telling you it's going to be worth it.
I can't stop thinking about your smile,
The way your laugh warms me,
Your arms wrapped around me; I felt safe.
No one else will have me like you do;
No one else will have me, only you.
There may be more guys in the world,
But I tripped and fell for you.
I'm falling too fast, don't let me get hurt.
When I told you there was someone else;
There never was, I just wanted you.
We both committed the perfect crime;
You stole my heart and I stole yours.
You're the type that is worth fighting for
No matter what.
If I had a penny for every time I thought of you,
I'd have one penny, you never leave my mind.
I can't tell you why I love you;
I think I was just born to.
I don't know where I'd be without you.
The only nightmares I get are about losing you.
I never thought I'd love you so much.
I know I'm in love with it's hard to say goodbye.
If I had to choose between loving you and breathing,
I'd use my last breath to say "I love you."

Jessica Ensell

It's a great honor to have my poem published and a great achievement at the age of sixteen. I have to thank my family and friends, especially Justin Beiber. He makes it seem possible for dreams to come true. He gave me the strength to believe. My English teacher, Ms. Erika Thomas, thank you for helping me find my passion for poetry. Thanks everyone for believing in me. I know it's got to be hard to support someone who downs themselves a lot. But everyone's worst critic is themselves. Love you guys!

Another Sleepless Night

Another sleepless night
Staring out my window
I can't get you off my mind
Tears falling on my pillow

My nights, they are so lonely
I need you more than you know
Wanting you here beside me
Oh, Lord, I love you so

I want to lay by your side
When we both say "good night"
With sweet dreams in mind
Holding each other tight

I want to wake in the mornings
To see your sweet smile
Hear the birds sing with glory
Kiss your sweet lips for awhile

Watch the sunrise together
Each day of our lives
Live life with you forever
Build memories with time

We'll share a love with each other
A love that is cherished each day
A love so precious and treasured
For the rest of our days

I've never felt this way before
I've searched forever and a day
You're the one I've been waiting for
I'll love you always, come what may

So open your heart, let me inside
I promise to love you 'til the end of time
Come, be with me, set your fears aside
I cannot bear another sleepless night

Wendy Jo Myers

Life Is Like a Garden...

I have a green thumb for just one reason,
I can always tell a live branch from a dead one....
Wind or rain or sleet or sun, any time, any season.

I wish that this talent extended to real life...
It would be nice to look you in the eyes
And know...
Are you a live wire, or a dead soul?

I contemplate these thoughts of self as I gaze into a beautiful spring sky,
And bear witness to a moon more full than I have ever seen.
My soul is scourged clean,
And ghosts flock around like moths...

The things that occupy my mind
Are out of sight, and out of time
And I'm well out of line.
I can't see straight, yet somehow I am fine....

But boy this getting old shit sucks. Looking back,
Ruminating on what you had, expiring for what you needs must....
But oh well, we're out of luck, stuck...
It's the price we pay just to die another day.

We all want one thing in this life...more time.
To do over...to do again...

Well that's too bad. The eternal damnation of mortality is to want
what we can't have,
No matter the eventuality.

Life is like a garden, a bone yard shaded with daisies
And memories best forgotten.
I tell myself to move forward, and remember I am alive
Not dead underground and rotten.

Bella Sanford

Cycling Season

Autumn mists dance in our presence, gentle whispers of silently
blowing wind blows our leaves in masses upon masses, carpet layers
clinging to the ground.
Whispering winds, clutches feathered gushes, bundles into piles.

Patches of twilights night quills breezes, sweeps aspiring in our silent
spaces.
Falling, falling, like feathers amongst the gigantic old swaying oak trees
now lay dwindling in the night of darkness wraps us in its web of deceit.

Tiny patches, sun glisten droplets, sheets of white snowy ice
meets with wintery branches, overhung in white cloudless slumber.
Silence entwines in warm embrace, sunless skies left far behind.

Fire burns brightly in houses made of stone smoke chimneys bellow
cloudless skies, wintery droplets, makes way for puddles in the ground.

Beauty rebounds, birthing into tiny new bubbles
springing buds dances blossom, spring slowly onto lighten branches
springing, springing, noises now upon our silent nights.
Slumbers finally left behind, hears our birds are calling.

Summers whispering tunes, grace us with its presence.
Glowing orange ball of fires, weave across our burning sky
changing, dancing, burning leaves on gentle branches.
Summer sunshine's comes a calling to all those restless nights.

Falling, falling, our cycle of seasons comes a calling, wrapping us
in tiny embraces, till night and day begin anew and fall aspires to come
a calling!

Carol Lynn Swenson

I have been interested in poetry and words for some time. To aspire is to create words from the heart. To annech is to inspire others to follow your lead. I am an Australian now living with my husband, who is American, in the States. Renewing my passion of poems is an ongoing pleasure.

To Those Who See, But Never Speak

Lift up your voice,
You deserve to be heard!
Don't be afraid —
Open the floodgates of your very essence,
The sole reason of your being within
Demand their respect!
Command their attention!
Whether if it's whispered or shouted,
Bring them forth
Grab a shovel; dig deep into their buried graves
Wield the power of emotion
Peel back the layers, one by one,
Opening their minds to the real world outside
Allow them a long glance in the mirror
Introduce them to their reflection of what-could-have-been
So heed this advice:
Lift up your beautiful voice,
For it's finally time you were heard!

Courtney Mayer

Paths of Life

Walking,
Running,
The destination is unknown.
Lost in faces, places,
Trying to find a way home.

Two roads lie ahead,
One of light,
One of dark.
Which path will be chosen?
The choice is guided by your heart.

The road of light,
The fate of good and wise.
The road of dark,
Bringing evil and demise.
Light is the heart's way home.

Rebecca Krawzik

Unsure

If I could say to you what I wish to say
I would not be left unsure.
Something holds my words inside.
Is it fear or something else?
I wish I said these things when I knew you.
But that is a regret I will have to live with
Until I find the courage to have them spoken aloud.
For now I have my pen and an endless supply of pages.
Pages filled with false beginnings and untold endings.
It is frustrating to have so many beginnings, empty for they
Have a middle and no last word.
What was it?
Is what I wish to say.
A question so long left unanswered.
And now I wonder if you know at all.
Are you at a loss as much as I?
We did not speak as I wished we could.
Too much silence in a place where the walls have
A tendency to close in on you.
The sense of it all escapes me because there was no rhyme or reason.
Funny for I so love my chaos.
I'm a contradiction really, for I love order as well.
I have strayed from the point I fear, for I know not what to say.
I don't think I ever knew.

Lauren Franklin

Pen Paused

Pen paused above a blank page
because I feel nothing, no joy, no rage
not one thing to write about
nothing comes to mind
so I doubt
I'll ever be able to make sense of this mess
and all that does is cause more stress
I need answers and inspiration
but all I've got is procrastination
so when I write is it no good?
Am I doing it like I should?
Is there even a right way?
I don't believe so,
'cause I say
the words as long as they come from within
are all you ever need to win
and in the end
start over again
make it better, stronger, with more feeling
write down all the things you are dealing with
and then...
Your story will shape itself in the end

So go on celebrate
it's your time, it's your date
to finally get some words on that page
and bring back the joy without the rage

Sara Karl

World Peace

Reaching towards the expanses of blue overhead
lost in the deep blue sea in the sky
thinking of how insignificant one person really is
comparing oneself to a universe infinitely bigger than oneself
putting ones power really into perspective
can one individual truly improve such a corrupt world
to fix the mistakes of the greedy and lazy
promoting humanity as a good thing and not a plague
improving the days of all that pass seems like a tall order
maybe a simple smile and a hand shake is a start
shaking hands with ones who are known
extending out to help the ones who need it most
to inconvenience oneself to improve somebody else's day
a nobel concept and a future goal
to think world peace may actually happen someday...

Matthew Wilsman

Simple America, living in the midwest. I grew up in large family north west of Chicago. Currently I am employed at Follett Library resources in Matleny, IL as a technical support specialist. My hobbies range from cars, music, writing, reading, video games, sports, and medical company. Poetry has become a focused way to present my thoughts, concerns, and opinion into writing for sharing with friends and fellow readers.

Wings

I'll send you my silver wings
to bring you to the place
where my heart longs to sing.

I'll bring you to the place
where you'll be free
For once you'll be safe.

And when darkness falls
I'll unfurl my wings
and protect you like fortress walls.

I'll soar into the night skies
and bring you back a pair of stars
to put in your eyes.

I'll slow down the rising sun
until your nightmares become dreams
and your fears are over and done.

Whenever you feel afraid
I'll unfurl my wings for a shield
I'll protect you from any shadowy raid.

And even though our love is forbidden
and its difficult to fight
you're the one who keeps me driven.

Carmen Pienaar

I was born and raised in South Africa and it was my mother who suggested that I should write my thoughts and feelings down. What started as rhymes and visions became escapes and a talent I'm proud of. I was fascinated by angels and that inspired me to write this poem. I'm not only a published poet, I'm also a published author of Swan Girl *by Published America. I hope one day to be called a best selling author and become a screenwriter for movies. I hope to keep writing until my brain and fingers can't work anymore.*

Dream Tree

My life is a tree,
Each dream a leaf.
Some will bud
And never grow,
Lost to the fears
That threaten them all.
Others will grow
Then shrivel and fade,
Torn from the tree
By relentless winds.
Yet enough will grow
To be all they can be,
And when my life is complete,
My tree will be full,
Dripping in color
In hues of hope.
For that
Is the color of dreams.

Kestra Bartholomew

I love poetry. The way one can express any idea, thought, feeling, or belief through the simple tools of pen and paper, finding a voice where one is difficult to find; all this I find amazing. I am only sixteen years old, but I know I will be writing poetry until my hands fail to hold a pen and the words' only escape is through my lips.

My Love

My love it seems
Is lost to me
For the time we live
Is strange and lost
Where love
And lust
Cannot be distinguished

For if this is love,
And not some propagandaed feeling
Even then we'll be forgotten
Lost in the spaces
I am nothing to him
Nothing more than an acquaintance
There is no "He and Me" and no "We"

For if in this time
"He" and "Me"
Became "We"
We shall love
And have love far beyond our years
For if "Love"
And "Lust" is separate
Or if there is a fine line
We shall have the truth
That lies within our hearts
And within ourselves

Mysti Skye Mullins

Eternity

You've no idea what you give me
My heart has never felt so free
I'm here for you and you for me
From now until eternity

I'm very special in your eyes
To me that is a big surprise
For you see something I don't see
You see deep down inside of me

I see the same within your eyes
Between us both our future lies
You care so deeply from the heart
I can't believe this fresh new start

Unconditional love we give
A life so new for us to live
I'm here for you and you for me
Together for eternity

Judy Maydich

Season's In Love

Springtime when everything
Becomes anew
It's the way I feel
Every day I look at you
It's a silly little crush
It's a feeling only I can touch
Before it becomes summer
I remind myself and wonder
Where would I be
If he never came back for me
Would I be the girl I am today?
I look back, and I understand
When true love grabs a hold of your hand
The Autumn leaves change
Just like your life
In love forever
He has made me his wife
Now that we are one in the same
Our love grows deeper
With every season's change
In winter it's cold, a playful delight
He snuggles me tightly on cold stormy nights
It's springtime again I hear the calls
Of the doves
Summer's heat gives me his undying
Season's in love

Claribell Ramstrom

Let Go

Let go

Let go of what you are trying to hold on to.
Let go of what you are hiding behind and just. be. you.
Let your true self, your spirit be as it is to be.
Can't you see...

Let go

Let go of the drama and calamity...
Of all the things that you are using to hold you back.
Let go of the crutches you cling to which disallow yourself to fully emerge.
I promise you won't crack.

Let go

Live for you and what God has planned.
Let go and take that stand.
Let go of forbidding yourself to shine
Let go of exclaiming... you are not mine.

Let go

Stop punishing, chastising, penalizing, rebuking yourself.
Come home and rest
by letting your guard be gone...
realize you have the Divine within.
You don't have to keep fighting, and pleasing, and hidin.'

You just have to...

Let go

Kathleen Lafrenie

Triumph of a Legend

Cristiano Ronaldo dos Santos Averio
A name so unforgettable, he's such a hero.

Born in February to a cook and a gardener,
He has the ability to move like a tiger.

Even the touch of his foot on the ball
Makes you want to love it all.

Call the soccer field his home
and the net his best friend.

He will destroy anyone who comes in
his path to steal his victory's blend.

Ronaldo makes soccer look simple
while dressing his team with glory.

When he's on the field,
soccer becomes his life story.

He's a legend among us so powerful and unique,
Changing the world by his mystique.

Sara Baig

Hi fellow reader, my name is Sara Baig, a sixteen-year-old girl from Toronto. I have always had a deep passion for poetry, as it allows me to express my opinion in the most creative way. Poetry enhances the ability to amplify my voice for things I love/care about. With this great honor of publication, I will continue to live my very blessed life and one day hope to achieve the title of a doctor. In the meantime, my hobbies include photography, gardening, volunteering and spending lots of time with family and friends. Forever a young-at-heart teenager.

To Be or Not To Be

He is always here for me
All say our love should be
I don't believe so, no I don't
I wouldn't date him, I won't

He is cute, I am not
Even if we've been through a lot
We are best friends, it will stay that way
Maybe, just maybe, until one day.

Destiny Turner

My name is Destiny Turner. I am twelve years old in the sixth grade. I love writing poetry. It may be a love-inspired romantic poem or a poem relating a darker side of myself or others I care about. Some of the facts may be true, some facts false, but they all come together to form a feeling within me that has to be expressed. I love to write poetry and let my feelings come alive on paper.

I'd Rather Be...

I'd rather be a tiger,
Prowling, and pouncing, and murdering my prey.
Showing off my strength, boasting about my power.

Let them be as deer, innocent in the brush.
Seen as weak, pathetic by all predators.
They never act, so we feast.
They simply run from their killer.
They simply hide in their terror,
But never to any avail.

To be the ruler, to make them quake in fear,
I live for the feeling of triumph when my victim
lay dying on the crisp, red ground.
To cast my shadow over the gazelles limp form,
I feel my reign renewing itself.

And to hear,
Oh!
To hear the scampering padded feet of the tiny creatures running.
They comfort their young from the death of their father,
As I enjoy my meal.

To be sought for my cunning striped.
To be sought for my intelligence.
To be sought for the cubs I father.
To be sought because I create fear.

I'd rather be a threat to the weak,
Than my prey greeting Death.
If I had to choose, I'd be the orange and black,
Than the fur streaked in red.
I'd rather be a tiger,
Claws, teeth, and all,
Looked upon with fear, and left alone by terror,
Than a squeamish creature hiding from what I am.

Morgan Giraud

Takers (Part II)

How can I be loved? How can I be forgiven?
He has stolen all from me, all
that was mine, and now my dignity, it is lost;
cannot be reclaimed, cannot be found again.
It is his. I will never be my own, for
from the outside in, he has robbed me of even that.
I am guilty, hang my head in shame, gravel pounds
and judgement passes. They do not know, cannot know;
but it haunts me, and I cannot escape.
But there are others, and we can stand,
together, we can stand against the Takers. We
unite in heart, though we do not know, have not met,
but we make each other strong, and they cannot,
no, we will not let them take anymore.
Our sin of vulnerability has condemned us,
not age, nor race, nor sex has defined, but
this one thing: we stood alone, undefended,
but now we stand together against them,
against the Takers, and we know
we have not lost the battle.
They, the Takers, they are the guilty, and we,
the Taken, shall be the victors, no more shamed,
tormented, degraded, unlovely by their hands, lust, sins.
Indeed, the war has just begun
and when it is done, we shall stand,
no longer fallen, but risen above and triumphant.

Kimberly J. Heide

Writing is a way to share one's voice, and poetry especially accomplishes that. I wrote this poem, the first part of which can be found in Best Poets and Poems of 2011, *as a way to speak for those who cannot. Child abuse is something we all need to be aware of and speak against and I am thankful that God has allowed me this opportunity to share my burden with a worldwide audience.*

Yesterday's Kiss

Yesterday's kiss was as real as it seemed,
Even though far, I still could taste it—
Those sweet, honey, sugar-like pillows, so kind
Those lovely and sexy lips of yours, love.
Those dark charming eyes were sparkling at me.
And your voice full of empathy stuck in my dream.

I cannot explain what I feel deep inside—
I delight your melodious voice
But I'm petrified of the lie.
I love looking through those dark charming eyes,
But I'm aghast that they might hide some secrets inside.
I've wanted your kiss for centuries long,
But I'm concerned if I go there, I may not return.

Yuliya Stasyuk

The Little Play Room

Little toy dolls and spinning tops
The sound of children's laughter
That never stops

Smiling clowns with their noses of red
Books of fairy tales waiting to be
Read

Little stuffed teddy bears, sitting on
The shelves so high
Waiting for a little girl's hug as the
Years pass them by

A toy train that still sits upon the
Track
Waiting for a little curly-haired boy
To return back

Just a little play room up in the
Attic high
Filled with precious memories as the
Years have gone by

Bobbi Jo Hager

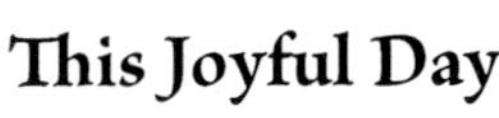

This Joyful Day

This is a sunny, happy, joyful day,
From early morning, sun rays gladly play,
Dark clouds were fast whisked away from this place,
A clear horizon gladdens each kind gaze.
A carefree folk
Left homes—everywhere people talk,
Have fun, laugh at the jokes, sing sincere songs and walk.
Blue heavens send
Their smiles, delighting all the land,
And everyone we meet seems like our dearest friend.

Again, as in youthful years in the breast,
Your heart is beating without any rest.
Anew with joy every time, your soul sings—
The ceaseless light of Dreams and Troth, it brings.
Some turquoise shine,
That's so unique and really fine
In our interminable huge world—yours and mine.
And love in sight
Always and everywhere—this bright
Sense gives birth to insuperable nerve and might.

For all our songs, there is a great demand—
They are performed by almost each jazz band!
It is so pleasant now—please, look, my dear,
These tender people's smiles flash there and here.
You have to beam—
When they go away, these days dim,
Yet everything will come true like in one good dream.
So, walk ahead—
Forget all that was bitter, sad.
To the nice future, hopes and faith have surely led!

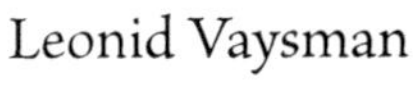

Leonid Vaysman

Untitled

In a suit made of metal
Lies only your brain.
You'll lose all emotion
To the cyber reign.

Don't you dare
Close your eyes.
If you do,
You'll surely die.

You won't remember them
Once you look past.
Silence will fall
When the question is asked.

Count the shadows,
Keep your head.
If you have two
You'll soon be dead.

What we need is a doctor
To save time and space.
The only one left
Who can save our race.

Emily Del-Sali

No Sympathy in War

I am not someone to placate your loneliness,
The sacrifice that you've made me.
Not a sheep left to be slaughtered
By the blades of your misery;
The kindness that you drained from me,
This blood so permanently lost.
I am not a soul that you want to manipulate;
The arsenal of these words,
This bulletproof tongue...
Don't underestimate them,
Not even for a second;
I'll be your demise so fast,
Your head won't have the time to spin.
Lock and load,
This means war;
A shot heard around the world,
This battlefield called love.
Choose your fate.
Stand with me,
Or forever wish that you had;
I may be broken,
But I will NOT be damned.
You want this heart back?
You're gonna have to break in.
Pick the locks that you so stupidly made,
The one's you so hurtfully caused me to create;
These iron bound defenses,
This master's lock.
Redemption is within your reach,
And this is your one and only chance.
So bottles up, baby,
Take a swig if you're nervous.
Break a sweat, baby,
There's no sympathy in war.

Vincent Cuccolo

Dear Poetry

Dear Poetry,
Why does my heart outshine the stars,
when you creep inside my dreams?
Dear Poetry,
Why do your problems make me emotional?
Dear Poetry,
When you tell me you love me,
why do you wait to the fifth stanza,
and not fifth line?
Dear Poetry,
Why did you disappear from me?
Dear Poetry,
I saw you hiding under quarter noted,
in between four-letter words.
Dear Poetry,
I've heard you're famous,
and you've come to be heard,
every time your host's lips part.
Dear Poetry,
When you flew across the crowds
and came to my attention,
our hearts became one again.
Dear Poetry,
ever since then,
I've been missing you.
If only Melody,
your stepfather,
didn't always overpower you,
beating you until your silent!
Dear Poetry,
I overcame your mother Acapella,
as I spoke of you.
Dear Poetry,
she misses you...

Sharice Fulton

I love Poetry. It only really started to impact my life two years ago. I loved the emotion a speaker had when they recited a poem and Mya Angelo inspired me as well with her poetic bravery. Then as time went by I would get so overwhelmed with poetry that I would write poems on the back of tests and quizzes. My science teacher finally told me about a group called Teens With a Purpose. They have a poetry group and within that I thrived on poetry. I enjoy writing. Hopefully one day, I'll make a difference all around.

Perfect Imperfection

It makes me disgusted to hear through the days
that certain people are "gods" in their ways
For these are the people who claim to be perfect
While everyone else carries every little defect
Now I am here to end all this hullabaloo
To tell all these "gods" that we're perfect too
Everyone's beautiful in the light of the morn
Everyone has talents that others adorn
We're just degraded by all of the rest
All of the people who think they're the best
It's time this must stop, so I ask all of you
Show off your protection, let it ring true!
Let no one hinder it, show it, scream it, let it spark!
Let no one get you down with their uncanny bark!
Take down your courage and pride; take it down from the shelf!
Wear it all proudly, and just be yourself!
For you, yes you are perfect in every way
No matter what the conceited might say

Sebastian Tame

My Son

Memories of another place and time, come to me and fill my mind,
thoughts of you when you were small, when mom could catch you
should you fall.
I lie awake till the morning sun, wondering, "Is there something I could
have done?"
What I would give to turn back time, to feel your tiny hand in mine.
To cherish and to hold you close, to protect you from what harms you
most.
Embedded in the soul of me is where you will remain to be, and while
I'm here I want to say, Yes, I loved you each and every day, and when
my time on earth is done, I will say to you "My Son"—
the privilege was mine to have been your mom.

Melissa House

When They Love Another

The heart craves a partner
To share in happiness and tears.
Do not become a prisoner
And wait through many years.

That curious, strong emotion
So often sung and written
Is really just a Siren,
Tempting those who've yet been bitten.

Longing for another's heart,
An often endless plight,
Retreat may at some time take a part,
But for now you ought to fight.

Gina Carra

Gina Carra is seventeen years old and aspires to be a film director. She's a cinephile and proud! Stories are her passion and words are her tools. "You've seen my name on the page of a book, now look for it on a movie screen!"

Solar Eclipse

Roaring wind calls.
The war begins.
The sun sits in his throne,
Feeling threatened.
The glistening moon
Glides to the sun.
She skirts, arches forward.
She gently kisses her rival,
Blocking his light from the world.
Leaving, the moon smirks,
Knowing for a second,
She had won.

Samantha Bryant

My friends call me Sam and I am fifteen. My favorite things to do are read and write. I want to share my poetry with promise. My words are always a discovery, but never a dream. My goal in life is to graduate college and be a therapist for abused and neglected children. I love my friends and cherish my family.

The Unbreakable Wall

The walls begin to quiver
as my heart starts to shiver
The pain slowly rips away
leaving behind only the darkness to stay
No more hope, no more light
only tears and fright
Crack! Crack! The bricks start to fall
Keeping me pinned against the wall
The pain digs in, as I realize
I'm alone again
Looking for an easy way out
as my body begins to shout!
Somebody please, stop the pain
for the sorrow devastatingly reigns
Band! Bang! The bricks crash to the ground
slower and slower my heart steadily pounds
Less and less I feel my breath
as I wait for the eternal rest
To one knee I do fall
for here goes the unbreakable wall.

David W. Gunter

Forty Some Odd Snowflakes

On waiting for the tourists and snow to fly our way,
sharp scissors to white paper, we passed the time of day.
When forty some odd snowflakes, the windows we did grace,
but who should then appear? Santa smiled upon your face.

"A prayer to the Snow gods, each waitress here has done—
or more, Dear, I've done four—can you guess but a one?"
You looked them all around the windows and the doors;
you looked me in the eye, until you looked no more.

But walked up to each snowflake, each one that I had done,
and pointed them out carefully—yes, every single one!
"There's that one in the corner, and this one here most near;
my favorite ones are that one there and this wee one right here."

You ask me why I love you; I don't know all to say....
So, think about the magic that you brought with you that day.
And know, Dear, that I love you—I scarcely need to try—
it's something that just is, and I can't quite answer why.

It's written in the snowflakes; it's written in the stars...
It's how I know that you are mine and know that I am yours.
It's how you knew instinctively which snowflakes I had done;
it's how I know that you, Dear, are my true beloved one!

Lisa J. Birkeland

Guardian Angel

Angel of light
Angel so bright
Wherever you are
I know you're listening
Ever since I was young
You were always there
I've always believed
That you'd be there for me
Even if I can't see you
I believe in you
Angel of light
Angel so bright
Watch over me in the night

Kaitlin Thern

Stars in Our Hearts

Stars in our hearts
Shimmering to break free
Showcase of arts
From poets like me
Uplifting and inspiring
For the joy that they bring
Great Poets Across America
Full of literary beauty
Great Poets Across America
Listening to the call of duty.

Florance Steele

The Internal Battle

I hate who I was
I hate who I am
When I think of how I've acted all I feel is regret
This life has become a game
How long can I stay?
How much longer can I drag myself out of bed?
How much longer can I put a smile on my face?
It's hard to survive when you hate yourself far too much
You lose the will that you once had
You lose the courage to live
You gain the courage to die
Your thoughts overtake you
Before you know it you're overpowered
But by whom?
Your thoughts have consumed you
They've taken over
And they won't set you free
Because the truth is
There is no escape
When the monsters live inside of your head

Nicole Norfolk

Nicole lives in Erie, PA with her dad and two brothers. She is currently in her junior year of high school at Mercyhurst Preparatory School. Nicole enjoys rowing for her school's crew team and dancing at Little Dance Studio. Nicole studies jazz, tap, modern, ballet, and hip-hop dance styles. She also enjoys listening to music and traveling. Her favorite band is The Maine. Nicole also enjoys blogging in her spare time.

Haunting Eyes

Oh glorious, beautiful eyes
Look upon me one last time
Show me the wisdom
You have received
Show me the delight
You have beheld
So dull now
With age
Torment and suffering seen
Your eyes will linger
Forever in my mind
For they are now
Only a dream

Laura Farley

To write is an amazing feeling. Poetry is my way of letting out the feelings held in my heart. I am so honored to be featured in a poetry book for National Poetry Month! Thank you and I hope you enjoy!

I Remember

I remember how it felt
to love the cards you're dealt
to live in a fantasy
to have your heart melt.
I remember how I believed
that you would never leave
I was blind at the time
but I would soon see.
I remember how you lied
I remember how I cried
when you walked away from me
you left me barely alive.
I remember all the pain
I couldn't even say your name
I remember how it hurt
it may never go away.
I remember how it felt
to hate the cards you're dealt
to live in a nightmare
to have your world melt.
I'll never forget what you did
I'll never forget how I slid
into a world of complete darkness
and how I stood back up again.
I will never go through that
it was my first and my last
I am a different person now
you are now only in my past.
I remember how I cried
how a part of me died
how you almost ended me
I remember.... How I survived.

Karly Parker

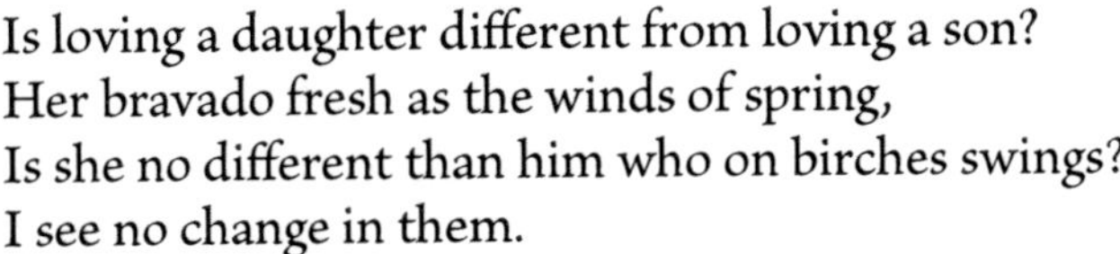

To Love a Daughter

Is loving a daughter different from loving a son?
Her bravado fresh as the winds of spring,
Is she no different than him who on birches swings?
I see no change in them.
If you do not count the years of life,
The falling of her petals as being the same.
Is she not as radiant as when she was but a baby?
When her hair was but peach fuzz and feet were as supple as silk,
Was she not as lovely?
Maybe, maybe the stars still envy her.
Do not all women stare at their reflections day in and day out
Envisioning where they were?
Is loving a son the same as loving a daughter?
Sprouting forth from the mother's womb,
The delicate fruit of a blessed act,
She, too, is far different than a son.
But do we not love them the same?
Her image, the dissimilar colored queen,
A card with a diverse shape, is a queen not a queen?
It is one family, all alike.
Is she not justified to crawl,
Deserving kisses when her legs get scrapes
And can she not speak as a son would
With enthusiasm and wit of an owl?
Everything a son can do she too could.
Ergo, stars, ergo, grass
Is loving a daughter as different as loving a son?

Rose Mae

My name is Rose Kathence Mae and I am a recovered anorexic. I am a woman and I am strong. I am the proud daughter of a hard working man and a virtuous woman. This poem is our statement to a world struggling still to accept women. It might be surprising to you, then, when I say this tiny nugget of truth. I am not a feminist. I stand for truth. I am an American and my heart rests in equality. Writing is what I do and with a pen, God willing, the world will hear my roar.

Memories of Symbols

Stinging, sliding slowly across the silky skin,
the meaning runs deeply.
Colours collect, like calligraphy, the collective conscious decisions
made on that fateful day.
Symbols selected and scratched onto and into my body mean.
They mean, not only to me, but also to my memories, those many
magnificent moments where time forever slows to a halt.
Pictures fade, memories slip away, but these meanings only grow.
Grow in size, design, intricately spreading a meaning across my being
until, when the light shines on them, I am the meaning.
I am the design,
the art,
the symbol of acceptance,
that still escapes the grasp of many who search for it.
Why do they do it?
Won't they regret it?
What does it mean?
The answer is that it does mean.
It means and matters, abstractly representing those moments in time
where memories, manipulated as they might seem, mean.
Staring, silently saying behind me that I will regret my meanings, are
those who do not want to understand my symbols,
my meaning.

Joe Letriz

I Rise

I rise,
The world is divided, so confused in this place.
Time is levitating like the objects of matter in outer space.
Memories are remembered, past life forgotten.
Present day is difficult and the future isn't spoken.
From the words that I speak to the thoughts that are in my mind,
God parted the clouds to let His children have light to shine,
So I rise.

I realize temptation is divine,
Through the lies in one's eyes,
Determination to keep hope alive,
And my struggles to perish and die.
Still I rise.

A man is underneath this skin.
Through thick and thin, I've had my heart misplaced like a skull with no skeleton.
Life moves slow but yet I know
The concepts repeat like a soft melody,
Convicted of being murdered in love so you can call my case a felony.
I survive from the tears in my eyes.
Why do I cry?
Then again I reply, "I am a man."
This means I take the subject of the matter into my own hands,
Plan to remain still and stand,
Never fall until the Lord calls.

I see…finally, not Donell Jones, but I know "Where I wanna be."
To be anything,
Take on everything,

Obstacles I climb while taking each step one at a time,
I rise.

Darius Robinson

Poetry has always been a way I can express my feelings and opinions toward the real world as well as in my life. I'm nineteen years old and a sophomore in college at Troy University. I love expressing my mind in my poetry because I feel that my audience can relate to my words and be lifted in enlightenment. My poem "I Rise" basically shows me maturing from a boy to a man without giving up hope. I hope readers feel they can "rise" as well no matter how hard life gets.

Would You?

If you were I and I were you
Would you still question the things I do
Would you finally understand the things I say
Would you finally see why I am this way
Would you see and maybe even feel
That all of this pain I'm in is actually real
Would you look back at all you've said
Would your face maybe get a little red
From all the guilt of what you've done
Hurting me, just to have a little fun.

Charity Bishop

It's All in You

As true as thunder is to lightning
So is that of your dreams and heart
As true as rain is to a rainbow
So is that of the beauty that you
Pass on the inside and outside

With the persistence you embody
So comes all that you desire
With the passion that lives within you
So comes the brightest of spotlights on you.

Along with all the faith and love you
have for yourself
Comes your dreams knocking at your door
Along with the joy and happiness you show life
Comes the belief in you from the heavens above

Jennifer Calabrese

Have a Little Faith

Oh hey darling, what's on your mind?
I can read your face like it's telling me a story.
You've been going through a rough patch
and it's been so long since he's been gone.

Oh hey darling, just let those tears fall.
Don't you ever hold them bottled in,
cry your heart out because you want to
and it's been so long since he's been gone.

Oh I know that you missed him so much.
It seemed like yesterday he was just here,
holding your hand and whispering into your ear.
You would give anything to have him back,
and to just to hear that sweet, old voice say hello.
Well, it's a little too late but just have a little faith.

Oh hey prince charming, what's been getting you down?
You seem to frown more than smile.
She was your everything, your world
and you just want someone to love.

Oh hey prince charming, just put on that smile.
Put all your sadness behind you in the past.
Hold open that door just for her and she'll smile
and you just want someone to love.

Oh I know that you missed her so much.
It seemed like yesterday she was just here
being there for you and saying "I love you".
You would give anything to have her back,
just to hear that sweet, small voice say hello.
Well it's a little too late but just have a little faith.

They met a few days down at the coffee shop in town.
She was wearing her dorky glasses and
reading a romantic novel when he approached.
That sweet, old voice said hey.
That sweet, small voice said hello.

Oh they dated for a few years now
till that one night when he pulled out a ring.
He got down on one knee and she said, yes.
From that moment on, she'd always smiled
and he'd always said hello.
Well, it's not too late to have a little faith.

Valerie M. Haag

Persephone Reincarnate

In Hades' solitary palace,
A legend through me has been reborn,
Now I'm forever bound to a life of malice.

A poisonous pomegranate stings my hand like a thorn,
Bloody tears pool at my swollen feet,
Frightened by my captor's scorn.

Demeter's cries to the heavens no longer discreet,
My mortal lover lost to his own grief,
My rescue a priority to the Olympian fleet.

Happiness to me now is like a crushed leaf,
My heart longs for his with an ache,
Hope no more a belief.

My sacrifice to save him my heart does break,
Suffering a consequence of a decision,
A mother's ignored warning a wrong path I do take.

Suffer I do now as dreams are an illusion,
The forbidden field I mistakenly frolicked about,
Not heeding advice as freedom is my delusion.

My soul's mirror forever devout,
Not knowing of my retched flaw,
For I am reincarnated as princess of death and doubt.

Kathryn Caldwell Smith

For as long as she can remember, writing has been Kathryn's greatest passion in life. An avid poet, Kathryn has been involved in her high school's literary journal for the past three years. She was recently published by the World Poetry Movement, and hopes to spread her love for poetry to others. Kathryn will be attending AZ USA Pacific University in the fall, where she will study to be an English teacher. Kathryn dreams of becoming a novelist, but in the meantime, hopes to share her love of the written word with future young writers. She would like to thank her parents for all of their support and love, and thank the Lord for this wonderful gift. Psalm 139

Gone But Not Forgotten

As for today it's only been a month
But the tears keep wetting my face
The whole family misses you so much
We're all asking God please say it is a mistake

Our boys are asking why you left so soon
With so many things left to do in life
You have no idea how much you're missed
How many of us just want your face to kiss

All our memories are being compiled for the kids
None of the kids had enough time as they should
Any pictures, anything of you to save it just for them
Oh I keep begging if only something I could

Could have done different, could've done harder
All we have is what ifs and left with no answers
I know how strong of a person you are
But without you now, loving you from afar

I hope you can see this and know we love so much
To only be able to say one last thing to you
Be able to see a smile, to hug onto your body
But most of all, we all miss your wonderful touch.

I have so much else to say
I guess I'll have to save for another day.
You are greatly miss Steve Walters Jr
And even loved a whole lot more.

Dee Walters

After losing my soulmate and father of my four children, I decided to put more time into my poetry writing and of course spending all the time I can with my children to assure them I love 'em with all my heart! I also let them know this mother of theirs is strong and not going anywhere for a very long time! The tears still roll and the why's still asked but I do my best to answer their questions and wipe each tear that falls down their beautiful cheeks. One day all of us will get better and the memories of us as a family will get to be more enjoyable and time for laughter and smiles. We will all get there in due time when we are ready.

Untitled

Hidden in plain site.
No one understands me.
I hide behind these clothes and this hair.
My new friends don't know the girl I am.
As I look at the mirror all I see is the
boy I'm hiding behind.
But maybe he will see me for the girl I
really am.

Mandy Winzenried

Tell Me

I look into your eyes and see the fire.
And it will not leave you, ever.
The wondrous look of your desire.
It will stay with you forever.

Denying its existence is not clever.
Trying to hide what is clearly shown.
Tell me now or tell me never.
The passion in you has grown.

Tell me what I have already known.
Tell me that you love me.
So my heart will be yours to own.
Or please darling, set me free.

But I may still love you with all my heart
Even if we choose to stay apart.

Tell me....

Kayla Williamson

Poetry is the one way I will always be able to express myself. All of my poems are straight from my heart. It's as natural to me as breathing. And I am greatly honored to have my work published. I hope everyone enjoys reading this poem as much as I did writing it.

Maze

I wander amid the forgotten corridors,
Remembering what was,

breathing, smelling, tasting the past,
intoxicating my senses.

The walls become paper, every word illuminating,
waking every consciousness in my soul.

I become the story, and the story
becomes me.
The labyrinth is clear to me now.

Such a profound stirring of my mind,
seeing everything and nothing at all.

All that I am is now just a dream...

Liane Lefler

The Father's Artist

The Father called to Ariana,
"Child, I need you home today."
Ariana answered,
"Lord, I'm on my way!"

"I need another artist
To paint the morning sky.
So you see, I need your help, dear,
And your life on Earth must die."

"I thought I'd have a future,
But You've said it isn't meant to be.
So I'll be painting pictures
In Heaven eternally.

When you wake and see the sunrise,
I hope you see my special touch.
I want you to see God's beauty,
Because I loved you very much.

So, Mom and Dad, please don't cry.
God meant for this to be.
I'm now the Father's artist,
In Heaven eternally."

Julie Jansen

My niece Ariana was sixteen when she died in an alcohol related motor vehicle accident. In my grief, my thoughts turned to her younger brother who had yet to realize that his big sister wasn't coming back home. I knew Ariana's death couldn't be in vain, and knowing how inspiring her own artwork was to us, I wrote this poem in remembrance of her. " The Father's Artist" was read at her funeral, and I still shed a tear when I read it. She will always be remembered and always loved.

Is There No Future

Is there no future
I wonder as time takes its hold
with troublements so impudent
while times of hardships that passed
But life goes on and on.

While problems everywhere rise
With somewhat suspect
But can we really believe our leaders
As we go on through life
With signs so low to trust.

As unemployment is so high and rising
With companies closing doors and moving to faraway lands
Because prices are cheaper
For shipping the things needed to ship
And keep their overhead down.

Can we care for the old
And give them their needs
Or will we suck their medical care dry
As we try to bring our debt down
Or maybe zap social security out
To pay our heavy load of bills we have.

Will our children feel restless
Because school safety is blink
Or will fears be small
As security is alert
When the crime rate rises.

Will the veteran families ever feel the love again
Of their husbands, wives or their children.
Though I know it is for our safety.

Will we ever feel safe
As we rest our heads on our pillows at night
Against so many evil frights
From faraway enemies or here at home.

These are things I surmise
And wonder if
Someday America will still stand strong and free
Or is there no future.

Ivan Zender

The Pass

Over the view is the time of day that the tomorrows bring before us.
Stop to look, seek to find the cross to the path of the road.
Before the stop, look against the side of the trees where the moss
grows... the direction is before you. Wander slowly as in the desert
pass no man shall ever see, as the travel is slipped easily and the urom
down cross is narrow. Tread safe the distance, the water is close beside,
never shall a rook be lost, safety is beyond the beginning.

Jo A. Davidson

The Storm

It's as though you can feel it coming
Like you can feel in deep inside
The clouds begin to thicken
You just want to run and hide
The chill in the air makes you shiver
The sun that was once shining bright
Now peaks through the clouds like a sliver
It's coming fast you can't control it
A storm like no other
Your body filled with fear
So close you can taste it
You close your eyes as it draws near
The thunder rumbles, your body shakes
You feel as though you will break
You wonder how much
Can your heart really take
Things start to spin out of control
You look around, you want to run
But which way should you go
The pain you've been through
The weak moments in life
The air feels so thick
You could cut it with a knife
This can't be the end you're not ready for this
You've fallen down before, you've broken in two
But you get back up
And keep pushing through
Life is tough; no one said it was easy
Here it comes, brace yourself
Keep your head held high
Stand in the rain, stand your ground
Stand strong when it all comes crashing down
For you will survive
The storm we call life

Angela R. Farmer

Last Words in the Diary of a White Witch

Last night I saw him standing there as he had before but
He was gone when I awoke from the dream.
Only his touch and embrace remain in thought.
Some say his ship was lost at sea but today it is anchored in the cove.
Tonight I will surely rendezvous with him.
I long to journey to the endless deep.
I long to cross over to the other side.
All enveloped in eternal stillness.
Time has set me free
But the abyss hidden in morning shadow is widening.
Only his love will break the spell of enmity's shadow.
The gray outline of dawn has given way to early sunrise.
The life I once knew is gone. I'm ready to join him.
I recall the words to a song I wrote long ago;
Its melody like the sight of the rising morning tide envelops me.
Let me be with the one who loves me now,
The one whose ship lies
Anchored in the cove below the crimson horizon.

Gail Logan

Think

Think of and do
Love, healing, deliverance
Memory
Remember
Remembrance
Think huge
Live LARGE
Awaken to a new call
Think not on earthly things
But do and think on things above
Do the work of Him
Who strengthens us
That His will be done
On earth, in our lives

Andrew L. Lewis

A Love Poem to Eternity

You are the wave that pulls the boy under,
swallowing him into the sea,
and the dance of two lovers barefoot
on the tiled patio at sundown.

You are a soldier belly down in the dirt
with his finger on the trigger,
and a mother holding a flag
folded thirteen times close to her heart.

You are a classroom of eager children
waiting for the anticipated sound of the bell,
and loved ones surrounding a hospital bed
when the last breath is taken.

You are the words "I do" exchanged
at the alter of a small country church,
and the first smile on the face
of a young couple's infant daughter.

You are His saving grace.
I want your endurance to finish the race.
I long for the optimism
to keep the smile on my face.

To look through your mirror
and reflect the past, present, and future,
and to use your strength
to carry the burdens that life unloads.

Georgianna Doepper

All About Her

Her eyes are so kind and gentle
Her smile is so sentimental
With just a touch I'm paralyzed
Her kisses leave me mesmerized
Her beauty makes me tremble to the floor
Her love makes my heart soar
With just a look she takes my breath
Never will my love cease, not even in death

David Hayes

Poetry has made a big impact in my life and getting published is one of the greatest things that's happened to me. This poem was actually something I wrote for my friend and his girlfriend and the inspiration come from their feelings for each other. But it also has meaning to me because it's in my opinion the best poem I've written.

In Between

Look up, look down
Wings spread, fluttering, or
Huddled, safe in a cocoon
Getting high off life
Staying low from its blows
Out in the open, embracing risks
Down in the comfort of darkness
Surrendering to sporadic winds
Taking comfort in the stillness
Free-falling into inevitable change
Hesitating to break free
Looking down at isolation
Looking up at true freedom
Looking up while crippled by small spaces
Looking down while soaring through opportunity
Soaking in energy from the sun
Satisfied with the moon's glow
Taking deep breaths
Just inhaling to survive
So I ask you
Am I flying high or
Is it the opposite
Am I too blind to see
That you are the one
Reaching down for me
Stuck in between
The butterfly in her cocoon

Rosa Rodriguez

Writing, in general, has always been one of the many loves of my life. Poetry is a lovely art. Every poem I have written has been like taking a deep breath after having realized something. After finishing a poem I feel it needs to be shared. Every poem is a look into the person that I am. Every poem I write gives the reader a specific perspective of how I see the world, of how I see myself.

My First Love

My first love
I felt in a moment of abundance

A bittersweet moment
Where I realized
How precious I am
How valuable I am

My moments in life
No matter the ending

I surpass all obstacles
I make the best of everything
I stay fabulous in my spirit
I learn from my mistakes
I keep positive in my mind
I am gorgeous in my body

My first love
Is me

Love means
I accept who I am
I believe in me
I let nothing stop me

My first love
Is me
And that's all I ever need

Ayeesha S. Kanji

Hands of Time

The hands of time
are ticking
Evil is still kicking
The world is so very deranged
Let's save
what can be salvaged

Tick Tock Tick
The world
is very sick

Big change
will come soon
we're not fully doomed
Time for change
to get
her way

Tock Tick Tock
She's chained
with a lock

Save a girl
who'll change
a world
Save a life
who'll stick a knife
in endless strife and grief

Tick Tock Tick
The world
is very sick She'll get her way
and then one day
life will be okay
No vanity or insanity
just sit
and wait for the day

Tick
Tock
Tick

Jade Sanchez

I have always loved to write. It has been a way for me to express myself positively. I may not be great with people and being social but I know I'll always have my ability to write. And look what great things came out of it!

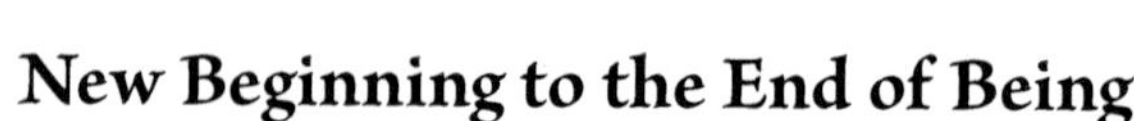

New Beginning to the End of Being

I had adorned myself and was running to meet you
I was welcomed by your marriage procession along my way.

I was putting together bricks of our little home
I am now gathering shreds of my broken heart.

I was hoping to have smiles glowing over my face
I am now drowning with my tears without any grace.

I was waiting for a ring 'round my finger
I now await a noose around my neck to linger.

I was beading a necklace of pearls for my neck
I have lost all the pearls and grace thorns on my neck.

I was hoping to wear a wedding gown from you
I now wish upon a scarf to be my shroud from you.

I had been dreaming of a beautiful life together
I have now got stab wounds on my heart offing to recover.

I was waiting for my new life to begin
I now wish for an end to my being.

I am alive with a hope to leave my body
To have your glimpse for the last time on my wake.

Was this your means of showing me love
Or was this your means to destroy my soul?

I could never hate you from the core of my heart
But I will love you for moments without the hurt.

May you be happy in your world of dreams
While I seek solace in the nightmares to come.

Rupel Patel

I was born in Kenya (east Africa) and have been living in the United Kingdom for just over ten years. I have been writing poetry in my spare time for some time. I derive immense pleasure from expressing myself through the written words. I have no prior training on the inner workings of poetry, but my inspiration comes from when I was much younger reading William Shakespeare's Romeo and Juliet. *I am delighted to discover that my words have been chosen to be published in this historic edition. I hope my poetry gives as much joy to the readers as it gives me to write.*

This Little Locket

I'll wear this little locket that holds your picture dear
Here around my neck where you are always near
I will wear it always so I can be with you
If I can't have you darling this locket will have to do
I look upon your picture that means so much to me
I will wear it always and watch you constantly
I can see you smiling I know it's just for me
Here in my locket together we will be
The chain that holds my locket is gold and shines so bright
Your pictures in my locket you're always in my sight
You'll be here forever, 'cause I love you so
That is why you're with me now no matter where I go
You're here in my locket, together we'll always be
You keep on a smiling, I know that smile's for me
You'll be here forever 'cause I love you so
This little locket goes with me no matter where I go

Ernestine J. Lee

I am a widow and am seventy-seven years old. I live in Daytona Beach, FL. Author re: A Girl Named June *by lst/books, re:* The Beginning of a New Dawn *by American Publishers. I have also been published in nineteen anthology books. I hold eighteen editor's choice awards. I belong to the Poetry Hall of Fame for writing spiritual songs and poems and am a member of the International Poets Society, of Cambridge Who's Who, as a VIP for my writings. I hold three diplomas—business, art, and decorating. I hold many silver and golden certificates for my writings. I was also named best poet for the year of 2000. I have a Golden Life's Membership to Chapel Hill Recording Company for the ability to write songs. I have put music to a lot of them and sang them in many churches. I am retired, now a landlord. My work carries three names. Recently I was put into* Professional Woman. *I've been married three times—Tebo, Bridge and Lee. I believe everyone is a poet by heart, to become one, they must write what is in the heart.*

Poem of Life That I Fight for Every Night

Life is life you fight every night. Here I am being myself in every fight that I live for. I hate my life, but I have to understand why I am still here waiting to die. Why do I cry every night? Do I have to fight to stay alive or do I just die? I may fight one last time, but I may not die.

I might have to live another night in my life that I fight. Being myself is not that light, but it is my life. Well here I am with one more life to live the Lord has given me. It is the life that I now live, the life that is reborn. I am now standing here looking at my lifeless body. There is a bottle of meds near me. Is that what took my life last night? Or was it my own fright that faithful night.

Gust D. Makres III

Hi, everyone. I have been writing poetry for eight years now. I am twenty-four years old and I love to write poetry; it is a great way for me to let everyone know how I am feeling at the time, and also to cope with the hard times in life. The story behind this poem is a true story about my life. When I was little, I was taken from my dad and put with my biological mother. She had a boyfriend who was always trying to kill me. When I was nine, I was run over. I was really hurt, having to fight for my life. I could not walk because I was disabled from the waist down. After six months, I was able to walk again, but fell going down two flights of stairs and was disabled again. The doctors told me that I would never be able to walk again. I did not give up the fight. I worked on walking and six months later, walked again. I have now been run over nine different times, and I am still alive. I never gave up on life. I had to fight for my life every night and every day. I have now joined a church and now I am able to help others in their lives to understand that life is worth living, and that there is a reason for everything that happens in life. I have had a rough life, but I know the Lord is watching.

Beautiful

As I look at the sky so blue
I can't help but think of you
the beauty that I saw that day
forever in my mind will stay

I see that beautiful smiling face
where in my heart will always have a place
A smile that sets your face aglow
it brightens my day I thought you should know

A smiling face that will never frown
your beautiful smile cannot be turned upside down
so keep that smile in its place
and never let it leave that beautiful face

So when I look at the clear blue sky
I will see your smiling face in my eye
A smile that will brighten a cloudy day
A beautiful smile that will forever stay

Joe Pippin

Here to Show Us the Way

Jesus was born on Christmas Day
Asleep in a manger on a mattress of hay
His birth was made known by a shining star
That could be seen both near and far
Here to deliver peace and love,
Jesus truly was a gift from Heaven above
Let us celebrate His arrival on this day
For He was born to show us the way....

Sierra Plys

When I wrote this poem, my intent was to reach the lost so that they would know the only way to salvation. I hope my writing inspires you to love Jesus and let Him show you the way.

Change

You ask me why I cry
I point to the sky

You swear oaths that can't be unsaid
I shake my head

When you pretend to care
It rips another tear

You demand to be heard,
I shake like a bird

Wanting to stop it,
Yet all I do is sit

When it all comes down
I can hardly make a sound

Standing in the pouring rain
I wonder if I'm sane

Looking in the mirror
I hate to see her

A frail shell,
But no one can tell

All of that willpower
Gone like a twin tower

If my old self saw me now
She'd scoff and wonder how

I used to be sure of my destiny
Now even tomorrow is a mystery

Anna Bagoly

Broken Promise

I was standing there in the blistering cold
In front of a lifeless, unforgiving tombstone
Crying from knowing the reason its here

We were best friends, since second grade
Two individuals, who were never apart
And one day, something happened, that destroyed us both

She came over one day, tears in her eyes
And when I asked her about it, I couldn't believe
To hear she had been raped, by her drunk father

We took the story about it to my parents
And they looked at us like it was a joke
What they didn't know, was she was dead inside

A few days later, she told me it happened again
And that night, we made each other a promise
We would form a suicide pact

The next day, I stole my dad's safe key
Where he kept all of his pistols, from working as a cop
I opened the doors, and took his favorite one

We skipped school that morning, and took a walk
Through the cold city streets of our hometown
And both of us, had left our final words in a suicide note

We made it to a park, the one where we first met
Knowing full well, that this would be the place
Where we would say goodbye to a cruel world

It was a bright afternoon, with no one around
And we could see our reflection, in the gleam of the gun
And as we counted to three, I watched her pull the trigger

I couldn't bring myself to do it, after seeing the result
And my scream were muffled, by an overflow of tears
And I held her there, wishing she hadn't done it

"Here lies Emily Downs" was engraved in the stone
Flowers surrounding it, all covered by snow
And I let myself cry, because I broke my promise

I'll never forget her, the girl I once knew
And I'll never forgive myself, for not following through
On a promise I made, to my best friend

Nick Gilstad

This award is truly amazing. I never believed that my poetry would ever receive such praise. Just having my name in a book like this is truly awe-inspiring. I'm actually planning on writing a novel in the near future, and World Poetry Movement putting my name out there for me is unbelievable. If my work is ever published outside of this organization, I promise to give them some credit.

Order of Society

What has the world come to
Thinking wrong is right
And right is wrong
Society has taken the world
And flipped it onto its head
Taking everyone under
When one would do a thing to question authority
You shan't be seen again

Nicole Kieda

Mental Malady

They stare at you with vacant eyes
They say things that are not wise
A beautiful mind is what they had
But here is what makes me sad
A beautiful mind that will make you smile
Was once theirs for a little while
But then their smile goes away
For something goes amiss
As they slip back into their deep abyss
If only you could touch their hearts
And tell their problems to depart
How happy you and they would be
Can anything relieve their pain
Imaginary things — no shame
Those vacant stares would all be gone
A life of hope full of song
Would belong to them again
And you would have a real good friend

Vera M. Meney

Poetry is a way of expressing your most intimate thoughts. These thoughts may or may not be taken from real life. It can include real life, fantasy, dreams, speculation, hopes, desires. It allows the writer to express on paper what she or he may not say directly to persons. It is a release from everyday tasks. For me, it is relaxing and pleasant.

Summer

Cruising down the
road,
winding like a
tossed ribbon.
The sun rains light
down on us,
melting our hands together.
I reach out
into the distance
and pull the future
close to me.
We embrace,
sizzling kisses on
steaming skin.
Summer speeds toward
and away from us,
like sunglasses worn
in the
shade,
but I'll still love you
after sunset.
After summer.

Tess Stoops

Twig, Twine and Sole

This wooden trinket means so much to me
I wondered why and how it came to be
Let me tell you about this clever man
Of course, I admit, I was his very best fan.
He heats up the furnace with jet-black coals
And melts scrap metal to make animal molds.
Thin sheets of tin became pinwheels and such
Dustpans and utensils formed beneath his touch.
Whittlling at wood he'd carve quaint little toys
To keep me amused and away from boys.
He left us with memories of times gone by.
The snowshoes he made to walk through the snow
A wagon and sled for my mother to tow.
The wagon was filled with produce to sell
Refilling their pantry with food for a spell.
Despite calloused hands and deafened ears,
The retirement years brought rewards less tears.
He and Mom left the city and bought a farm
The poultry and livestock added much charm.
He'd sharpen his tools on a grinding stone
His tools and Mom's knives he happily honed.
The treasure I covet is kept in a safe
It brings one from sorrow to a happier place.
What's this thing Mom? She smiled and grinned
"A fly swatter." she said a bit chagrined.
"It's a shoe sole tied to a twig with twine.
To swat flies that buzz about and works just fine.
The twig holds memories of love so true
And I know it will do the same for you."

Elizabeth Williams-Medhus

Elizabeth Williams-Medhus emigrated from Vancouver, B.C. Canada in 1961. While living in Rolling Hills, CA, she worked as a medical office manager for her husband, Dr. Edward Williams. Elizabeth was actively involved with community and international philanthropic organizations and honored with Resolutions from the California State Legislature, Senate, and the "Women's Wall of Honor," at El Camino College, Torrance, CA. Since the passing of my parents and husband, I remarried Sigurd Medhus, who has encouraged me to write. It was through my cathartic writings that I realized how an insignificant object could bring one joy triggering many wonderful memories.

How Graceful Is Yours

How beautiful and graceful an orchid can be
Sweet and colourful can be
It smells like a sweet perfume
It carries love within its soul

How beautiful and graceful are they
To enter their world of love
I would do all I can to have my orchid's soul

How beautiful and graceful and orchid is
Sweet and happy in her life
The world could not harm her beautiful orchid soul

How beautiful and graceful are they
Happy with friends around
Surrounded by flowers like her
Full of life and colour
The colour of an orchid's soul

How beautiful and graceful an orchid is
Full of love and caring
The orchid is my garden's soul

How beautiful and graceful is she
Full of hopes and dreams
Growing to her soul
Growing in my garden
Its beauty to behold my orchid's soul

She left one winter night
But comes again in spring with her beauty
With the colour of her soul

My beautiful and graceful orchid
Here to say many things about her soul
Her soul of beauty, hope, and love
How graceful her soul is

How graceful is yours?

Easter D. Morgan

Your Guitar

The placement
of your fingers upon my neck,
and your core pressed
against my body
makes me sing.
Without you,
I am an empty tune.

No one
could have loved me more.
Cause you,
my rock star,
took me home
from that music store.
Amongst the walls
of instruments
is where I lay.
You picked me up,
held me once,
instantly knew that I
was to be yours.

We got home
you plugged me in,
turned me on
and began to play.
Our first song soon flowed
from the melody
we made.

Your voice
is my matching harmony.
When you sing along
with the chords you play
we come together as one,
as if marriage bound
by our musical romance.

Sasha Heikkila

The Storm

Trees dance in the boisterous wind,
Wind chimes clatter against each other,
My hair flips back and forth,
I look up and see the storm.

Flowers struggle to say rooted,
A roar of a monster breaks the calm of spring,
New leaves fall from tree branches.
Dark blue clouds overtake the last rays of sunlight.
Rushing back into my house,
I watch the world change from my window.

One wet drop lands on the front porch,
Two more on my mail box,
Soon, hundreds began to fall from the sky.
Rain falls in sheets,
Everything that wasn't covered is drenched
I watch, fascinated.

A loud boom shakes my house.
My cat runs and hides in my room.
Lightning lights up the sky,

I stay where I am.
Thunder slams down its hammer,
And lightning zaps across the sky once more.
Soon enough, the rain slows,
The lightning and thunder begins to fade.
My cat comes out of hiding.
The earth is cleansed again.

Melodi K. Smith

Love Gone M.I.A.

You were my first
And one true love.
When we would hug
Our body's fit like a glove.

But things have changed
And my love was altered.
I should have known
I would have faltered.

I love you, though
As my best friend.
Please say you'll stay
Forever 'til the end.

I am so sorry
To do this to someone so kind.
I wish you true happiness
And everything you find.

I dedicate this poem
To an amazing military man.
This wasn't how it was meant
This was never my plan.

I won't say "goodbye my lover"
Because that's not what I want.
Please don't ever hate me
Instead, our friendship we'll flaunt.

Officer Benjamin Jordan Nichols
You did nothing but love.
This is just a new chapter
We'll continue as turtledoves.

I love you!

Jessica Noel Wagner

I wrote this poem in a deep depression. My newlywed husband just left for the navy in March, and my heart broke. I love this man so much and have been with him for six years, but my love is no longer the love of a wife. He is an incredible man and deserves the world. I dedicate this to you, Officer Benjamin Jordan Nichols. I love you! Stay safe.

My Best Friend for Life!

Some things never change better just let
them be. My best friend he never knew
the challenges life would bring him his
own paradise drowned in his mind of one
day breakin' free. My best friend is quicker
than the ray of light he once told me
I shouldn't care what anyone thinks
of me, he said I have to cry tough,
my best friend the one with the blonde
hair and blue eyes once said
just be you and that's what counts
when life gives you bad medicine you
just have to take it! My best friend once
said you have to keep the faith. He said
love yourself I'll be there for you!
Come to find out my best friend is like
me, my best friend not anybody else's
my best friend forever always had the
best advice!

Jessica Duke

In the Night

As I lay cozy in bed around midnight,
I hear a burst of air and awake with fright.

What could have stopped my slumber,
Now fear builds as I wonder.

Perhaps I left the window unlocked,
A thief stands still and to me mocks.

Perhaps a murderer climbed through,
If that's the case what should I do.

What if it's not a man at all,
Perhaps it's something cute and small.

What about venom and disease and such,
The possibilities are all too much.

I glance at my cane filled with woe,
I can't wait forever let's go.

With one quick movement I fly out of bed,
The way I swung my cane it'll be dead.

A crash and bang the villain ceased to be,
Quickly I turned on the light to see.

What I saw in light gave me a shock,
My cane stuck in a fan there it mocked.

I killed my fan the monster in the night,
My imagination gave me the fright.

Ronald Eayre

Invisible

When I go out in the world without my hearing aids on
No one will notice that I cannot hear and understand.
    It is assumed that everyone can hear
    So no one is aware of me lip reading.

They think I am just more attentive than others
Because I am focused and I am a "good listener"
    The truth of the matter is that I am deaf
    And without my hearing aids I cannot hear.

My hearing impairment or handicap is invisible;
My deafness is inside of me and it cannot be seen.
    There is no sign of me not hearing you with my ears;
    So I use my eyes to make out the formation of the words
    from your lips, teeth and tongue.

And after a while you may notice the frown on my forehead trying to make out what you just said,
Asking you to repeat the words you have just spoken.
    "Oh nothing, it wasn't important." Why did you speak in the first place?
    So you could hear yourself talk? Or is the silence too much to bear?

I am deaf and yet I "act" like I am a hearing person.
I try hard to keep up with the hearing world.
    I am stressed out and tired because I don't want to be left behind
    With the news and happenings of the sounds around me,
    especially words that are spoken.

"Oh nothing, it wasn't important." This statement crushes me and
    builds up mistrust in me.

Why do you speak of words without meaning?
My deafness is invisible and I don't take it lightly to waste words.
It takes energy to connect and belong.

It takes skill to lip read with the help of people who understand speech;
And I have learned to receive hints and advice of how to bring me up to speed of what is going on.
I am invisible and yet you believe that you "see" all of me.
And no, you do not see "all" of me.

My hearing impairment and deafness is invisible.
It will remain that way until you know me.
Connect with me and take time with me to see your face;
For my eyes are my ears, and I hear with my eyes.

I am invisible until you find me seeing your face and you see me
And know there is something different about me.

Roger H. Dobitz

I lost my hearing at the age of two from the measles. I received my first set of hearing aids at the age of six just before entering school. I did not speak until I attended school with the help of a speech therapist every week for the first six years of elementary school. I dedicate this poem to those who help children and adults, who are speech pathologists, audiologists and speech therapists. They saw my potentiality and brought it out of me to share myself with the world.

Rumors

You can feel it in the air,
The anticipation, excitement.
Will they come?
No one knows.

His new mistress,
His new bride?
Will she come? Would she dare?

"I heard..."
"I heard..."
"I heard..."
Echoes through the halls.

"...she's unacceptable!"
"...she's inferior!"
"...she's a witch!"
Judgment passes over the unknown.

"Shhhh!"
"She's here!"
The mistress walks in,
Head held high.

She is beautiful,
Proud,
And ready for anything.
Not a sound is made.

He comes in behind her,
Takes her arm,
Whispers in her ear
He is clearly besotted.

No one says a word.
No one looks away.
Funny isn't it?
That rumors start this way?

Kayla Noelle Sakai

The Crush

He stares
Eyes like the ocean, blue with majestic grace
And his words speak clear and smooth
He smiles, and my heart does a dance at ten times its beat
He looks away, shy and embarrassed
My face turns a bright shade of pink and red
He looks back again
He smiles
But his smile goes right through me
To the girl, right behind me.

Erin Hantz

Mental State

My mind paints Dali images, sick and twisted
My mental state is ever drenched in colors of blood and night.
My wants are dangerous.
Like Spartacus, methodic with his vengeance,
I look harmless from afar
Yet my eyes are the doorway to hell.
Enter if you dare.

My heart is cut
Wounded and bound
Never to its original form.
Pieced back together like a picture puzzle, untouched
Like a family torn apart due to actions not agreed upon.
Things are not quite the same.

To speak is difficult.
My emotions always seem to get the best of me.
Cat's got my tongue, unfortunately.
Pen and paper... words spill out of my head like "word vomit."
Dark, lonely, yet beautiful and relatable,
Poetry is a sweet release for me.

Each time I write... I paint locations in my head.
Every piece has its home... all but one.
One is left in sanctuary.
Massacres there are none.
No pods of human remains to contaminate my holy ground.
Deep into darkest black forest my little cottage I can run,
Run to pour my pain and tears away.
Where all my secrets are kept.
Where no one can hurt me.
Where no one can lie to me.
Where no one can find me.
A place where I can just be me.

Mimi Quach

Still

One day in April, when the sun was still high,
and the weather was content with serenity in a sigh,

My family and I traveled afar to the Southern countryside
where more of us—in supreme abundance—reside.

To this end, we drew up our carriage, drawn by no horses,
to make up time already thus in losses.

As we plowed on through that day—
that time that people always forget to be pleasant and gay—

I kept myself in preoccupation through
the mere process of staring out a window.
I stared at the neighboring grass and trees that
towered and covered all in eventual patches of shadow.

I came to realize that all of that,
as simple as it was like staring out the window,
was—and always shall be—perfection—
a word that I now cherish in everlasting recollection.

But how is that so?
How was I moved so profoundly?

And then, as if in answer,
I remember how those trees had
blown to one side, then the other...

Now I remember,
the scene was beautiful,
it was calm—it was still.

Oh yes, it was as still as the sunset,
still as the smile of our Lord, still as...
my now learned, and eternally rested, heart from that simple day.

Content, myself, with that thought,
I start to look at that very same sunset, my oldest friend.

The only difference now, however, is that
the two of us are both now calm and complete...

The two of us, are now, in fact, forever still.

Anthony Cornatzer

Friends

Friends are just like gold,
Sometimes you end up with the fake stuff
And that brings you down sure 'nough.
But other times you find the real thing
Which makes you just want to sing.
They're with you through good and bad
And make you smile when you're sad.
Yes, friends are like gold,
And worth so much more when you're old.

Bryant Hirata

Looking Ahead

Look down at your feet,
Watch where they fall,
Make sure they meet,
The ground most of all.

Don't look forward,
Or else you may trip,
You were warned,
That you may slip.

If all this time,
Is spent looking at our feet,
How are we to climb,
And know where our future leads?

Less time should be spent,
Focused on the future, instead,
More times should be lent,
To looking ahead.

Rachel Bryan

On the Outside

I saw you stumble,
And I saw you fall.
I didn't know how to handle this all.

You cried all the time,
You said you were scared.
I never noticed how much you cared.

But now,
Now it's time to move on,
No matter where,
Know I'm there.
It's not that great on the inside
But honey, take it from me,
It's not better on the outside.

He said forever,
I guess it wasn't true.
But I saw how you made it through.

He took it all away,
All that you have worked for.
And he didn't even look back at the door.

But now,
Now I see you're moving on.
No matter where,
I know you will be there.
It's improving there on the inside,
And honey, from what I can see,
It's getting better on the outside.

That was then, this is now,
And everything seems to be falling into place
somehow.

Marissa D. Cafaro

Poetry, for me, has been a way to get my feelings out on paper. Sometimes I would write poetry and sometimes I would add to my log. I am so glad to have entered in the World Poetry Movement contest because not only do I get to show my talent in poetry, but I also get opportunities I thought I would never have. I am glad to introduce this new poem I wrote because I wrote it in dedication to those who have suffered the traumatic experience of a loss of a close friend of mine. Thank you for publishing my poem.

9-11: A Fitting Tribute

As the tenth anniversary was here,
I'm certain the victims' relatives still felt fear.
The newly named Patriot's Day,
Honours the fallen heroes in its own way.
Life has gone on since then,
The memories never fade given what happened.
A new sense of hope will eventually arise,
As dawn appears in the morning sky.
Terrorism is still being condemned today,
That will never change as the world has its say.
We paused to remember and reflect upon the terrible price paid.
These cowardly acts won't soon be forgotten—
That Tuesday morning the world changed forever and even again!

Marc Mullo

As someone with a disability, life is much more challenging; however having a strong support network does help. I am proud to be a Canadian and published author, with my first book just recently released, a collection of poetry might I add. I would consider my work more professional than amateurs, but it still feels gratifying seeing it in print or even online. My occupation and educational background as an author keep me focused and grounded for the most part. I study and work at home as well much of the time. My hobbies include camping and volunteering. Keep writing!

Five Butterflies and Counting

This urge, my old friend, my past demon,
Has come back to haunt me, to torture me.
I will not fall at your feet this time;
I will hold my head up high and fight you.
I can win this battle, if I try.
I don't care to lose my life,
Not to you, not this time.
I'm too strong for you to overpower;
You will never break this new armor.
Made of love, faith, hope, and dreams,
It may be ever-changing, but it still protects against you
And your different harbingers.
You make them more and more powerful,
Filling them with your hate and rage,
More tangible than you yourself are.
You may flow like liquid through my mind,
But you aren't, not yet,
Not until you get your way.
Then the liquid is warm, red, sticky—
It stains my life, my past.
My own blood, spilling from my body,
Leaves tear tracks on my face, soul, and body.
The deeper I cut, the less I feel—
Is it worth it in the end?
I will fight you, break these chains;
I'm taking back the life you took from me.

Victoria Seltzer

I've been writing poetry for about five years now, and it's my lie. This poem in particular means a lot to me because of its meaning. I am a recovering self-injurer, and the title "Five Butterflies and Counting" is based off of the Butterfly Project, which is where if you feel like self-injuring, you draw a butterfly on your arm/wrist. If you self-injure, the butterfly "dies." The day this was written, I drew five butterflies on my wrist and was considering more. This poem, in short, is about the battle a recovering self-injurer faces every day.

The Soul

I've wondered long and hard
About this thing called "The Soul"
It seems it has some magic
Which makes the body whole

I imagine God sitting there
In Heaven on his throne
Fashioning each and every one
As if it were his own

Making sure that each of them
Were special in their own way
Giving each a unique gift
To use from day to day

I see a loving God holding it
So gently in his hands
Stroking it with tenderness
Knowing exactly where it will land

As God surveys the women
He spots the parent to be
Ah, ha, He thinks to himself
I'll plant you inside "she"

The Soul nestles in the baby
All snug warm and cozy
Until that glorious day
When it comes out wet and rosy

Throughout the years the Soul
Computed every life detail
Transmitting them to God
Who keeps a lasting trail

Then when life's journey finally ends
And our time on Earth is done
God beckons for the Soul to come
Back to His Father's arms.

Frances Dampier

Frances Purnell-Dampier was born in Winona, MS, and grew up in the small town of Greenwood, MS. She is presently a retired educator after thirty-nine years of service. Frances taught English at Sunnyvale Middle School for over twenty years and later became assistant principal and principal there in the Sunnyvale School District. She was also the principal of Bishop Elementary School in Sunnyvale, California, for seven years. Frances acquired her bachelor of science degree at Jackson State University in Jackson, MS, and her master's degree in administrative services at La Verne University in California. Frances has successfully been published in two works of poetry. Her poems include, "Barack Obama" in Collected Whispers *and "America's Unraveling" in* Stars in Our Hearts. *Frances has three sons, three daughters-in-law, seven grandchildren, two grandchildren by marriage, and two sisters. She resides in Tracy, CA.* Cuddled in God's Hands: A Mississippi Childhood Unveiled *by Frances Purnell-Dampier, her new book released in April 2012, is a magnificent inspirational autobiographical journey of a woman whose life is filled with a mixture of joy, pain, tragedy, euphoria, and supernatural visions. This memoir portrays the author's upbringing in Greenwood, MS, during the pinnacle of the Civil Rights movement. During this turbulent segregated period in history, the author gives an in-depth look at her life and how, as a teenager, she and her family coped.*

The Truth Is...

They say I'm playing with fire
I say they're only burning themselves
They say I will never get through life
I say I will get farther than they've ever gone
They say there is a reason for why she's better
I say you don't see what she does when you're gone
They say I'm a failure and a disgrace
I say you don't know the real me
They say so many things but the truth is...
I'm beautiful, strong, independent and
perfect in my own way
So I will never care of what
They say....

Luisa T. Sanchez

When I write poetry I don't write about my personal experience, I write about others' experiences. I read a lot and sometimes I take an emotional experience from the book and convert it into a poem. I started writing in seventh grade and I loved books all my life, so I realized that I want to write as a living. In school I always have a pen in hand and scribble down a story, poems, or just plain phrases. So in a year's time writing became a way of life for me.

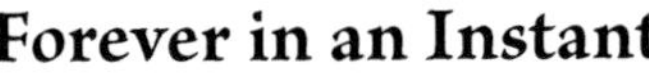

Forever in an Instant

Every day there is one thing I can't get off my mind.
No matter what I do or how hard I try,
it's crazy how just one look, one smile
can seem to stop time for eternity.
And in that very moment everything that has
ever mattered fades into nothingness.
As I stand there motionless, completely
mesmerized by your unrivaled beauty,
time stands still as I become lost in your eyes.
Seconds seem like days, minutes like years.
My heart starts to flutter the moment I
realize you are smiling back at me.
I can't help but wonder, did time stop for you as well?
Did your heart, your soul, your very being
just feel complete for the first time like mine did?
My body temperature starts to sky rocket
and my thoughts want to erupt like a volcano.
Despite my love of talking I continue to stand silent, still,
as if your very smile has stripped away my vocal chords.
And in that moment of infinite silence,
I finally find the courage to speak.
After going over it a thousand times in my head,
finding the perfect thing to say all that comes out is "Hi."
Even after saying "Hi," I still had trouble talking
continuously getting choked up.
The gleam in your smile, the smile in your eyes,
the soothing tone of your voice—it grabs
a hold of me and won't let me go.
And from that point on you're all I think about.
The only thing I look forward to each and every day
and the one I dream about being with for a long, long time.

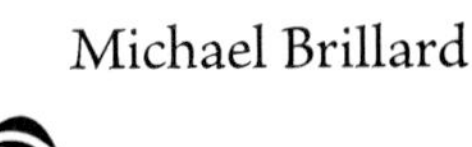

Michael Brillard

The Recognition

Ghosts of past
Follow one to death;
Where else can they reside?
A stranger to the crowd,
A painful memory to the letter,
He is the red thread,
The blood drained from an unconventional mother's heart.

Past loyalties lost,
Love that played pretend,
Warmth that is dead,
Gone with the child
Of harrowing lust.

Reckoning knocks
Open your door
Freedom only comes
After the past has been dealt
Her black hand of death

Don't shy from your open wounds, bleeding with the painful truth
One must go back to the prison door
So that liberty can walk through the window.

Hannah Dissinger

This poem is inspired by The Scarlet Letter *by Nathaniel Hawthorne. Inspiration is all around us and* The Scarlet Letter *displays that perfectly. Poetry is a gift, my gift, and I'm glad it can be put to good use.*

Stars and Stripes

What is so special about red, white and blue?
After all, they are just colors dear to me and you!
What set them apart from black, brown or green?
Yes, they too are colors, just like the others, proud of their gleam!
They are colors filled with hopes and dreams,
and if you don't understand, it's an American thing!
Red stands for the blood our forefathers shed.
White stands for freedom found in our head.
Blue is for the hard work opportunity brings.
To live in a country that has everything.
A land filled with rivers and fresh water streams;
Where you have oceans on each coast
and mountains in between.
Oh stars and stripes, how beautiful art thou!
This diverse land of abundance carved out by the plow.
There are people here from every walk of life.
Men, women and children, freedom as their plight!
Stars and stripes, oh how I love thee!
The land, the air, the ocean and sea!
Red, white and blue are colors, so it seems,
When you look closer there's much more meaning.
They are beacons of hope to people the world around.
There is no where else on earth, such opportunity found.
Stars and stripes, oh how I love thee!
The land, the air, the ocean and sea!
I pledge to honor you all my life,
God bless America and
The stars and stripes!

Regineld Shelton

Blood vs Flesh

Arguing will never stop,
mother and daughter at war
fighting for the right of reason
this can only go so far.

Clear blood running
out of mother's eyes
daughter fully loaded with ammo
and plenty of strong allies.

Trenches filled with emotions
that got released during battle.
All was forgotten in
what really matters.

Ending in bad welfare
daughter holds to power
that will be the end of
the first dying hour.

Kelli Magana

Hidden

To sway back and forth on the untamed sea, sitting on the bow of an unrestrained ship headed for my destiny.
Water as far as my eyes can see, its vastness fascinating and frightening to think of what might be.

Waves destined to cause anxiety over what may or may not be deep within me.
These thoughts haunt my mind, causing me to wonder over and over again like riding the waves of a dreadful storm.
Just as I believe I have finally crossed the brim, it all arrives again.

I only have left what is hidden beneath the surface, much too deep to find by looking through the murky darkness at more gloom.
Resumption is clearly not what is meant to be or somehow I would be able to find my way through all the disarray.

Trying to find those hidden treasures, pulling from depths of the unknown,
invisible are most pleasures, I can't seem to find all the buried jewels.
Concealed perhaps for protection, I seek the secret deep beneath.

Surely even I have something so profound it won't go unseen,
asking God to guide me showing me the only way.

Belinda Frank

Wandered

There is no one to dry your tears
There is no one to sing you to sleep
There is no one to check for monsters

There are no tea parties
There is no jester
There is no laughing or playing
or joking or dancing

You've wandered too far
You've wandered beyond

You'll have to find your own way out
But I must tell you I don't play fair
Yes, I will cheat
Yes, I will trick you
You must be clever and cunning
to find your way out

If you want to get back to your dolls
and to your home
You'll have to past my test

If you want to get back
to your mother and father
You'll have to pass my test

If you should not succeed
then you will have to stay
You will have to laugh and play here
This will be your new home
If you cannot pass my test

Jacquie Goodman

Forgotten Child

Prayer from a young girl
Momma's pretty darling
Daddy's precious angel
A baby made by forbidden love
Left alone, lost to a war of drugs
She cries into the darkened night
Forgotten and in destitute
She prays for another chance
Begs for the strength to go on
She looks to the ferocious night
Her eyes light in hope
As the Aurora Borealis flares to life
The clouds part to reunite
The piercing air takes her home
to a place she had once known

Tanisha Suzuki

Drown

Waking up,
at the bottom of the ocean.
Moving hysterically,
but still in slow motion.
Swimming,
as fast as I can.
Stretching to go further,
but still touching the sand.
Frantically kicking,
harder and harder I try.
Seeing the sun,
and kissing the sky.
Heart beating,
cutting to a stop.
One last breath,
I'm beginning to drop.
Muscles are weak,
body slowing down.
I reached the top,
as I began to drown.

Robynmarie Tavares

I Forever Will

Sweet kisses
Gentle on my lips

A warm embrace
His arms surrounding me

I love him

Angry words
Escaping our mouths

A single teardrop
Sneaking out of my eye

I love him

Words of apology
Filling the room

A silent understanding
Entering our minds

I love him

Forgiveness found
Gazing deep in his eyes

A simple vow
Promising our future together

I love him now
I forever will

Laura Steffen

Walking to School

Walking to school,
The days were many
And so were their toils.
Life was normal as it appeared
While its happening surreal as the seasons.
We were the school kids,
Some of us tough.
Others were the neighborhood wanderers;
Yet some more were destitute hostages.
Walking to school was tiring and endless,
Yet the garments didn't fit every kid.
For the most, the walk was a docile path.
Our needs were less and suffering was more.
Yet some parents eyed the distant future
Others didn't for reasons too big to pull.
But walking to school
Was never priceless or prizeless.
With the sun on our back,
Our feet ate their dust.
With the rain,
Our heads drenched in its pouring.
The cold penetrated our coatless bodies.
Despite all odds,
Our zeal embraced walking to school.
Breakfast and lunch was never a must.
One meal a day saw our stomachs famished,
So we scrambled and fletched
And eluded the injustices of hunger.
Walking to school -
Our covering-headline a non-fiction;
And the cure met battered faces.
Harshness embraced us on countless fronts,
Dried tears marked our faces with constancy,
Walking to school, yesterday's battle must win
And bring today's manifestation.
In retrospect, a realization pops.
Walking to school,
With feet to perseverance and commitment,
Yields no regrets today's world.

Charles D. Lamadine

A Daughter's Lament

My mommy, I come to sit by your side
For you are sick and I need to be near.
You have a sickness and I want to help you get well,
For you are my mommy and I need you.
I hate to see you sick. It hurts my heart.
You are usually so vibrant and so happy.
Now you just lie there sleeping.
Am I going to lose you?
Are you going to live with God?
I know He will take care of you.
He will make you well, but I don't want to give you up.
You have been the best mommy since I was born.
You have cared for me since I was born.
You have loved me and spanked my bottom when I was naughty.
I tried to be good, Mommy, yet sometimes I think the devil
did get hold of me. You prayed for me and kept me good.
I am here by your side, holding your old, wrinkled hand in mine
Trying to let you know how much I have loved you over the years.
I cannot give you much now, it is too late.
Soon you will be in the house of God.
He will love you and make you well.
I am sad, but should I be sad?
For he goes to prepare a place for you
In a mansion over the hilltop.
Your time is coming....
I will miss you, but I will remember
The good times we had, Mommy. Goodbye, Mommy.

Jeannie Urban

Untitled

If one shall come across a beauty
Then gaze at what their eyes behold
One beauty like none other face they'd
seen before
And when that beauty looks up at you
you realize now that they're much more
beautiful than you knew
And when you both walk away
their picture still in your head
you think to yourself
That beauty made you speechless
and what could you ever have said

Christian Hasler

Depressed and Curious

Depressed days and depressed nights
With no sun to shine, with no moon to look upon
The streets are quiet, the wind is calm
I wander around the house like a ghost

I've lost everything, nothing is left
So there shall be no light
I die in darkness, in coldness
Voices of demons mock me, laugh at my name

Living in this cursed life, and leaving my soul
To burn in the afterlife, destroyed by the fire of Hades
But I will not leave this place
Not until I'm forgiven for my sins

I wish I could do my life over
Curiosity didn't just kill the cat, it killed us all
The red button was pushed because of curiosity
The explosion was so loud and big
The city was wiped clean of houses and people
Luckily the explosion only went as far as the city border
But it was all my fault
I haunt the ruins of my once beautiful city
That was rebuilt five years later

I can't stand pain, all the lives that were ruined
My day has died sadly I am a breaking wall
This will go on daily, maybe I will leave this place soon
But I won't be alone for long, (a huge explosion happens)
See what I mean, curiosity didn't just kill the cat (joined by a little boy ghost)
It killed us all, and caused a long life of depression

Kyara Hampton

Black Beauty

All of a sudden all the light focused on her
I could see the expressed explicit intricacies of nature
But am not persuaded that it is complicated in any bit
I admire the curvatures gently carved by the Almighty
I could see beauty and elegant not begging for permission
So fascinated that my eye's aqueous humor dissolve every detail of this image sporadically
I am so puzzled by the fact that I could be counted worthy to find favor in the sight of this wonderful lady
My deepest inspiration to this spectacular damsel is not just her beauty but her very rich character that just reflects like the green grass so exuberant to shine
Her shining white teeth always flash a long lasting smile
Her eyes light up in delight as she shows her courage to assist and help you in any way she can
She is so hardworking but could I compare her to the ant?
I would say this will be a fatal underestimation
She swept me off the ground with her industrious nature and she wins by wildest admiration through her spring of love.
Her bosom is succulent with hope and her hands ready for the plough
With every trip back home I feel welcomed
Her humor set the place lit up like a candle
She is indeed a well of accomplishment for me, no wonder God made a wife to compliment a man as a helpmate
Well done dear God.
I love her with heart and I will do everything to show my respect for her
She indeed is one among a million daughters to me.
This is mine I mean mine.
What then do I say, we are one among a thousand.

Akwenuke Ofejiro

The Mask

Ah, the masks we wear
To keep our souls from being so abruptly bare
In contrast to the ever-changing emotions we must tame
A mask, truly, always remains the same

Wood: so hollow
So empty, pressed into its desired shape, so shallow
Crafted smoothly it blankly stares,
Guarding the delicate innards of our beings, it spares

We wear these masks to disguise these useless tears
For not everything is simply what it appears
Let the world not worry itself with our distress
One pain unheard is one pain less

What the eye sees beautiful surely can lie
But what one never sees one can always deny
To be blissful and serene is a difficult task
But for us, it is simple, for we wear the mask

Nadia Elamin

Beyond the Meager Flesh

What is it that makes us take the veneers, our most deceptive organ given us and insist it is truth? When it is no more than the ideal of face-value. Why is our judgment so quickly made based solely upon what is no more important than the tiniest speck of dust? Why can't this shallow habit be penetrated by a gust of wind and swept away like that speck of dust can? Is it because it has been bore and sewn into the very gray matter that acts as the mastermind of our being ever since we emerged from our mother's womb? Or is it society's grip upon the corrupt thought they very well created in us? Why is it that our heart only pumps the red life through us? Does it no longer see past the deceit we rely so solely on? Can't a beautiful disguise obscure the rotting flesh that hides underneath? Is it inconceivable that a lusterless veil be lifted to reveal the most stunning core? Why is it not that the inner is shown through to what is on display to the world? Will we always be held prisoner to our own prejudice? Or will we break free using finally not the eye that cannot see beyond the meager flesh but instead the heart that sees through the evasive skin into the soul where the true beauty is forever held, longing to be cherished for the treasure it holds just below the surface. For it is not of flesh that we are made but rather it is soul, love, personality, passion that makes us truly sublime.

Nikki Danielle Deforge

Crimson Roses

Well, this is how the story ends:
With you and all your razor blade
Grins, and me and all my two-cent
Friends who never heard of dying
For a cause. Or anything bigger
Than the back of their hands.

None of us ever looked ahead
For consequences. Never thought
that we'd be here when the
Curtain came to close. Just swam
Along through the stream, each
Pursuing another dream.

Too proud to meet along the
Shore, we all clutched our ill
Begotten dozen dead end roses,
Each the color of crimson.
Picked long before they had time
To bloom.

Left them on the stage when it became
Time to take our leave.
I took your razor blade and you
Took my two-cent friends. Parted
Ways to different shores. We can't
Stand to see us any more. Guess
That's what happens when
Crimson roses come into bloom.
There's forever a difference and a distance
Between me and you.

Gaylen Cook

I've been writing since I can remember. Before I even knew how to write my own name. I'd spend hours scribbling on a notebook and convince people that I was writing a story. That habit has stuck with me through the years. Though I'd hope my substance matter has improved.

Being Different

Staring at the mirror
looking into the eyes of
my own reflection

Wondering what other people
see when they look at me

How different am I?

Why can't people accept
me for me?

Having a difference in preferences
has severe consequences

You lose family,
friends, and even
the opportunity of finding true love

Just because they can't accept it

I learned to live with it
and hope they will too

As I look into the eyes
of my own reflection

I say to myself,
"You don't need to change.
Being different is never going
to be a bad thing."

Graciela Berenice Lopez

Ashamed

I'm not that perfect girl you make me seem to be.
You tell your friends how great I am.
When will this pressure stop?
Everything I say comes out in lies.
I wanna tell you the truth,
but it will hurt me if I do
and it will hurt you too.
I wanna be normal like you.
But I never will be.
I'm sorry.
I'm not that perfect girl
that you hoped I would be.

Sorelle Paige

All the writing that I do is directly inspired by how I currently feel. I write so I can release all my emotions. When I write, I am able to express myself in a way that I find hard to when talking to other people.

Need to Believe

You need to believe
In self-image of yourself
The person in you that no one knows about
The beauty of you
The life that is no other
A life that is different,
Different from all the others
Because being different
is what makes you special

You need to believe
In the acceptance of yourself
No matter what anyone says
For nothing could ever penetrate
The love you share with others,
Believe in yourself for yourself
Against the negative and with the positives

You need to believe
That love is the key
That makes us who we are
Love is the bond
That keeps friends together
For when you love
Others will love you,
It's the love of others everyone needs
That makes you real and eternal

You need to believe
In your heart
Because the flame of acceptance conquers all
For love means togetherness
I believe that we can make a difference in the world
By accepting ourselves for who we are
And loving others eternally
Whether you love or you hate
I believe we prosper from each other

Tyler Chinappi

Tenacious Love

My life is clouds
Black ones
You are the sun that clears the clouds after a storm
Tears will be tears and fall
Not a drop reaches the ground in your presence
I never knew what love was
You gave me that unforgettable knowledge
Your love is addicting and so dangerous
It could almost kill me, this addiction
This obsession
If you leave
Be sure to buy a shovel
Bury me.

Tiah Bright

Tears

Tears are sliding down my face,
Slowly gliding down in place.
As they slide down my cheek,
I can barely speak.

I sniffle and snuffle from in my nose.
The pain inside me slowly grows.
Now with anger and fury as well,
I wish it would burst and stop ringing a bell.

As my mom sees the anger in my eyes.
I try to let ii fade and die.
Sometimes I think of the bloody red scream.
But I push it away as a bad dream.

Keyara Aiken

I am fourteen years old and in eighth grade. I go to Cincinnatus Middle School. This is my fourth poem published. My first two poems published were in the books called anthology of poetry; my third poem was published in a book called Stars in Our Hearts. *Now I have a poem published in this book. I started poetry in sixth grade when my first poem was published. My first two poems were depressing and about saying goodbye to someone you love. My second one was about dance. But most of my poems are written out of anger or sadness. So most poetry I write is depressing. I wrote this poem one night when I was angry at my mom. I was expressing everything I was writing in the poem. Poetry means so much to me; it is a way to express my feelings and tell about my life. It's a way of relieving stress.*

Pink Is ...

You live to die,
It may be through the color pink.
Pink is hope.
You're strong on the inside and out,
You're getting weaker every day.
Keep believing,
You'll be alright.
You got family who love you,
Till the end.
Pink is hope.
Pink is love.
We all listen,
We all cry.
Don't give up on us,
We love you,
Till the end.
Pink is strength.
Pink is love.
Pink is hope.
Fight like a girl.
I love you mom.

Amanda Young

I love writing poems. My poetry is a very big part of me. Poetry means a lot to me. It's a way of expressing my feelings when I don't want to talk to anyone. When I write poetry it just has to come to me. I can't just sit down and write. I love reading other people's poems as well as I love other people reading mine.

My Therapy

I know who I am,
I just need to assemble all the pieces.
To make peace with this war inside me
Could mean accepting derangement
As genius.
Written in the sky
Born by the river
Trapped between my head and heart,
With the messages they're trying to deliver.

Until life unravels a therapeutic gift.
As bold, black ink comforts poetic screams,
Cleansing my soul,
Capturing beauty in imperfection
Resurrecting forgotten dreams
Liberating my unspoken voice
Preserving who I am meant to be.
To free my mind,
I find power in poetry.

After a prayer,
Healing starts here
With a silent melody,
Seeing reason in the unreasonable
Making sense of my insanity
Providing faith for the unbelievable
Enforcing my will to fight
Growing stronger
With every word I write.

Christian Danielle

When God Created Me

When God created me
He is the only one could see
Just what he had planned
to be, the story of my life
He spoke into being
one so free, to grow
to praise his majesty
Only he knew what you'd see
when you chanced to know
me as I am

He filled my heart with love to give
He gave my eyes sight the path to see
and a keen mind, and his word
my life to lead.
Trusting in his love
I can live, without fear
Trusting His words
I'll give others hope and cheer
For I know because He created me
In His eyes I'll always special be

So words of comfort to others
soft I'll give
To show his light and as
an example live that
they can learn of
salvations wondrous gift
I've learned He wants to be
my loving King and
that's just why He created
me

Joyce A. Yeargin

Lily Blossom

Lily Blossom you're so innocent and fair.
There is purity behind with all you share.
Your eyes tell a story,
They are windows glory.

Angels breathe sweet flowers,
Sweet things like the rain showers.
I imagine babies with angel wings,
Crying sounds like temporary singing.

Every day little angel blossom is content,
Nothing boring does she resent.
No complaining, by happiness she shares,
Eyes show excitement in all she hears.

Lily Blossoms, you make the world smile,
Angel wings you make my world shine.
Rainy days are scented wonderfully,
By my side you make my world sing.

Welcome to God's green earth,
Compared to time, money is of no worth.
No no, do not have one fear,
You are so loved, mommy is near.

Stacy Shields

Memories of Time

See this watch
my great-granddaddy gave it to my gramps on Feb 14th
See this watch
my gramps had it on the moment he pulled out grandma's ring
to propose
See this watch
my gramp's hand shook it nervously
seconds before he cut daddy's umbilical chord
See this watch
my granddaddy had it survive on his wrist
through two earthquakes, a revolution, and nuclear disaster
See this watch
they found it on his hand
the day he died
See this watch
though that day it stopped working
I'll still
and forever
wear it with pride

Clara Maria Mustata

Somewhere

I wonder what it's like to live above the stars
To breathe in the air of rich prosperity and to be touched by all that is great,
To sing childish melodies and reminisce on the times when eyes were smiling.
I wonder what it's like to live somewhere beyond
To play with doves that are glowing and watch flowers that are blooming,
To run with faces that you once new and listen to words that you once spoke.
I wonder when I'll live somewhere, somewhere that is above the stars and beyond.

Gabrielle Catalano

100 Years Ago

Icy water, piercing screams
100 years ago
Thousands dying, women crying
Temperature so low
I felt a shutter, I felt it hit
The iceberg passes by
Little do the passengers know
Half of them will die
The nearest ship is miles away
They will not make it before
The great ship Titanic
Hits the ocean floor
They said she was unsinkable
But boy, were they wrong
Their thoughts were not true
The Titanic wasn't that strong
Imagine clinging to a lifeboat
Fearing for your life
As men were cutting lifeboats free
With only a mere pocketknife
There are people screaming all around you
The tones of the crew barking orders isn't very nice
People jumping from the sinking ship
Into water colder than ice
That's what thousands of people experienced
This you now know
When the Titanic sank from underneath them
100 years ago

Alyssa Coleman

Is Justice for All?

America's open wound of turbulent history and divisive pitfalls
Built by immigrants, slaves, undocumented workers, heeding the call
Toiling to enrich life from their present circumstance and sorrow
Echoes of painful memories, unlocking doors filled with shame and horror
Justice is for the top one percent, the majority is void, recurring spiral downfall

A young man died two months ago after misinterpretation of a state's gun law
In a middle of the school week, on the edge of night after the day's warm thaw
Wearing only a hoodie, jeans, athletic shoes and the exuberance of youth
Gunned down by another who felt threatened by his racial essence of truth
His mother left bewildered never to hug his presence, hear his plans or thoughts

Where is the justice for this young man?
As his parents cry out for fairness in this land
History repeats itself, slapping us boldly in the face

Feeling of disparity, anguish, and oppression, little advance by the human race
A senseless killing another blemish against our nation's stance

Who can justify the murder of God's creation?
Willful stalking of men as prey while full of damnation
Is it about having skin that is black, brown or white?
What happened to civility and our sense of wrong and right?
Rest assured, on our demise, justice is proclaimed, too late for mediation.

Brenda G. Williams

Footprints in the Snow

Each set is new and unique…if you make them.
They are your very own…and nobody, no matter how strong or how wise can make them for you.
We survive by taking one step at a time…knowing full well if the steps are to be deep and profound they will only be as deep as the snow.
We can make the footprints as large and the strides as long as our legs will allow.
Regardless how great we think those strides may be, we find others that are able to take giant leaps, still others that have to run to keep up.
We find some of our children trying to follow each step carefully while others try completely different paths…some that we will never understand.
No matter how long or straight the path it may end far too soon, even before we have reached all our goals or the elusive stars on the distant horizon.
As our footprints fade into the melting snows we often become sad and despondent but we go quietly with the peace of mind that no matter how great or difficult the journey may have been, we will end up in the arms of God…if only…we believe!

Charles Sisson

Chuck was born in Englewood, CO, in 1933. After a brief professional baseball career he completed his baccalaureate degree (1956) and masters (1958) at Emporia State University in Emporia, KS. He was later awarded fellowships at Florida State and Colorado University where he completed his doctorate (1971). His career began as a teacher and a coach in Independence, KS. He moved to Winfield, KS, where he was eventually appointed assistant superintendant of Winfield Schools before leaving for Florida State in 1970. He then took an administrative position in the Boulder Valley Schools in Boulder, CO, followed by three years in the Colorado Department of Ed. He was appointed to a special position in the Gerald Ford Administration in Washington DC as an educational analyst. Following his public service he moved to the private sector at Battelle Memorial Institute in Columbus, OH; Electronic Data Systems in Plano, TX; and Oracle in Redwood Shores, CA. He finished his career as an adjunct professor at Texas A & M University in Commerce, TX. He has retired to his residence of the past twenty-three years with his wife, Paula, in McKinney, TX. He has six children, twelve grandchildren, and three great-grandchildren.

The Flightless Bird and the Buzzing Bee

I am in despair
because I cut off all of my hair.
I cut it off for you
and my secret emotions continue to stew.
I want to show you my love
in a fit of ecstatic passion
but my sober judgment reminds me
that such trysts are out of fashion.
I want to hold your hand in the sunlight
so the envious prudes can see.
They would gossip as they gape at us—
the flightless bird and the buzzing bee.
The social media would be rife
with the lurid breaking news.
Our "friends" would study the aspersions
so they could choose the proper views.
But we would have that day, at least,
and we should pray it never ends.
For true hearts ache when the sun descends
beneath the horizon's western bend.
'Cause on the morrow looms the consequence
for embracing nature's mirth.
The news will reach the ears of those
who buy and sell us for what we're worth.
Happiness is denied to you and me
because of what is and what never should be.

William Bryce Levanti

Mr. Levanti lives in West Frankfort, Illinois. He is currently a student, working on his master's degree in the field of education through Jones International University. Mr. Levanti enjoys to read, write and play music.

Eyes Anew

For many years my mind has been clouded.
I see now with eyes anew.
The sun shines brighter,
The grass grows greener.

It's all because of you.

Losing you was my worst regret.
The pain of it I shall never forget.

I was confused,
I was lost.

Most of all I was hurt,
Hurt because you had left me
With nothing but a memory.

The anguish was unbearable,
Seemingly un-repairable.

Then one day I remembered your smile,
Though I hadn't seen you in a while.

What I felt was not sorrow,
But a coming warmth for the morrow.

You welcomed the world with opened arms,
Knowing that you would never be harmed.
Knowing that you would have boundless love,
And be accepted into the gates above.

I remembered how you taught me to care,
For the people everywhere.
This is a vow I will never undo,
For now I see with eyes anew.

Susan R. Holly

I have been writing ever since I was a very young girl. Writing is not simply a pastime or a "fad" for me. To me, it is living, it is an urge that cannot be ignored. When I write I do it because I must. I simply have no choice. The poems I write are often spontaneous and raw, because I do so on a whim. It is an absolute passion. "Eyes Anew" is a poem that needed to be shared with the world, words that could NOT be kept to myself. It is dedicated to my Vova, my Grandmother, who passed away in early 2006. May her spirit live on forever.

The Ring

Close by the door he paused to stand
As he took his class ring off her hand
All who were watching could not speak
As a single tear ran down his cheek
Memories and moments as they had fun
Laughing beneath the shining sun
Remembering only his guest to be free
How he hurt her he could not see
Her warm brown eyes had grown cold
He would never again have her to hold
This special girl he sure would miss
He said I love you as he bent near
In words so soft no one could hear
The door has closed and his head hung low
As they carried her casket
Through the cold white snow

Stephanie Jones

Poetry to me is away to express the way I feel. Good mood or bad, poetry cheers me up. Poetry to me sums up everyday life. My father James Jones has always encouraged my poetry writing as well as my sister Tina Jones and my ex-husband Timmy Jackson. And for all their support I love them all very much. I hope everyone enjoys the poem. Thank you! I live in Fayetteville, N.C. I'm forty-three years old. I enjoy writing poetry and doing velvet art.

My Special Place

It's a dark place, as dark as the rooms in hell.
Though there's no actual flames.
The memories burn all around me.
Thoughts of my Dad and his family swarm me in this place.
I don't mind one bit because that's why I'm here.
To think about the damage that has been done.
In an odd way it makes me feel safe.
To be there in the bone chilling environment.
Although, it is very claustrophobic in there I don't mind.
It's the arm's length walls and North Pole temperatures
that make this my place.
All I see is the charcoal blackness around me.
It's a comforting look and feeling, no?
Some might say I punish myself when I go here.
I go for the sake of relaxing and nothing more.
The silence has an eerie yet comforting element.
It keeps all things clear until something appears.
When that time comes I just breeze through it.
Satan wants to hurt me, but this is my safe place.
My God gave me this place, and only I shall control it.
Disturbing thoughts may get to me at times, but I push through them.
Rays of sunshine will escape from time to time, but not all that often.
The darkness is more comfortable for me; I think better that way.
This is why my special place is my mind.

Brittani Gugel

Light-Hearted

I peered out the window, looking at the luminescent sky.
It was dark and almost too quiet, too still, too normal.
I pondered to myself, how loud and how bright it must be out there to others.
I then grabbed a hold of the locket that lay ever so lightly upon my neck.
I felt a quiet tear run down my cheek, knowing how important it was to be strong.
I cried not only for our soldiers so far away, but for my soldier.
For my soldier was left out there in a war zone, one of death and despair.
I clenched my locket as if it were a cliff and I was slipping, merely inches from the end.
With trembling fingers, I carefully unlocked the heart-shaped case
To see the photo of him, the last one I had to date.
I gazed for moments, trying so hard to bring my gaze from the photo.
It was impossible, knowing that at any moment I may not have him anymore.
I then looked up remembering that the moon was as close to a communication device as we had.
For I knew he gazed upon it, and I did the same.
It was a promise that we dare not to break.
I then carefully clasped my locket and placed it adjacent to my pillow,
Making sure it carefully reflected the light to give warmth to such a dark room.
Then before closing my eyes, I gave the locket a quick kiss,
Hoping somewhere, my soldier would know that I dare not forget about him.
The light-hearted promise was all that I knew to be true anymore.

Kerry Shaughnessy

A Careless Night

Shadowy, silent, starry night,
You hide night's creatures far from sight.
The ghostly gleam of which you show
only proves the fears that my heart does know.
Biting, slashing, hateful is your howl,
hiding beneath that is your icy growl.
Appealing your look, attractive your sight,
little we know of your unyielding might.
The life you give to the coming year
is shrouded, smothered by each frozen sneer.
Quickly we travel, tenderly wrapped tight,
hoping only to make it through
this never-ending cold, careless night.

Jack Everett Abernathy

Untitled

A spark of delight
dances in the golden orbs
of your eyes.
It lights the room on fire
and ignites my heart;
an incredible love for a child.
The undeniable innocence
reveals a smile;
a gift received.
A meaningless gesture
overtaken and embraced with joy
by an imaginative mind.
Showing kindness in its simplicity
as life truly should be.
Not taken for granted,
when a small spark
can start a fire.

Aleta Pierce

My Love for You

I know I will always love you
always be the sky above you
be your star that twinkles bright
in your life the shining light

by your side every day
in your heart is what I pray
I'll be the air you draw in
I'll be the prize that you win

I'll be the beat of your heart
of your day I'll be the start
always in your heart and mind
as our souls become entwined

I'll be the food that you eat
I'll worship you and kiss your feet
I'll be the strength of your arms
and the sum of all your charms

I'll be the darkness in the night
the answer to your daily plight
never let you leave my side
until everything we have tried

to always be a part of me
doesn't matter where I be
in my heart in my life
forever be my loving wife

Ronald Karzmarczyk

God's Breath

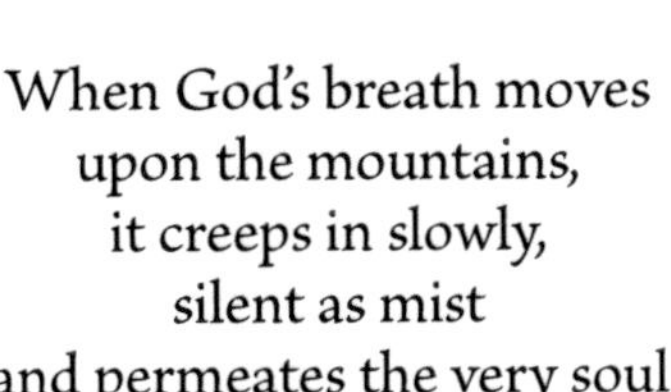

When God's breath moves
upon the mountains,
it creeps in slowly,
silent as mist
and permeates the very soul
with mystery.

It is like a cloud
that hides a secret,
a veil of silk
that covers a woman's
beauty.

And when it speaks,
it murmurs with a chorus of streams,
whispering of greater, unseen things
beyond shadows
of gloomy death.

It moves into the cracks
of all creation
and settles upon the waters of the deep,
as the starry firmament
opens up its dome
and scatters its many wonders
upon the glassy surface.

I am caught
between two heavens—
One
reflecting the other
my soul,
cloudy with God's breath.

Clayton Oberquell

Most of my poetry reflects my love for nature, and it often stems from an experience or place found in the wilderness of Montana, my beloved home. As an amateur photographer, my photos sometimes turn in to poems themselves as I try to relive the moments captured on film and express their beauty with words.

Dandelion Puff

Make a wish, my dearest love,
on a dandelion puff.
Blow it into the wind,
into tomorrow,
so that all your sweetest dreams
may come true.

I hope that you will make them live,
bring them life,
so that you may continue
to dream, to love.

Meagan Calhoun

I am very excited to be able to see my work in print. This is my second publication, something that I am very proud of. Writing is my passion and I plan to work very hard to get far. Thanks to Jennah, Michael and Misty, my mom, my grandparents, and Sandy. And, to the rest of my family and friends. I love you all.

My Friend

The softness of your voice
the beauty of your smile
the gleam in your eyes
brings these words from my heart.
One could search worldwide
and not feel what I feel deep inside.
A feeling of dignity and pride
when I call you "my friend,"
there be no treasure on earth
to measure
what your friendship be worth.
Let there be no end . . .
to calling you "My Friend"

Robert Garcia

The Nameless Poem

The invisible color you cannot see
Is the answer to everything
Within its walls you cannot breach
Lie the golden bells to ring
Through its dark tunnels' reach
Are the layers of Time
Never lost, never found
Waiting for the glories renowned

Logan A. Crowder

Turning of the Mind

I met a beautiful lady
A few years ago
A wonderful, loving mother
With countenance all aglow!
I visited her quite often
Sometimes, sitting down to eat
These meetings we experienced
For me a wonderful treat!
The days, the months,
The years have passed
And with this fleeting of time
Life has dealt this lovely lady
A turning of the mind!
Once, tending to the needs of family
Bestowing kind deeds on others
Today, on others, she must rely
Compassionate, caring husband and son
A loving brother and mother!
We wonder how could this be so?
That such a beautiful person
Should suffer in this life below
Her condition, over time, to worsen!
Our understanding today, unclear
As to why this had to happen
One day, the purpose will be revealed
Perhaps, when we enter Heaven!
Until then, we will ask the Lord
To give us a heart of understanding
Bestowing upon her all of our love
That, to her, we may truly be a blessing!

Donald E. McKinney

Donald McKinney is a retired North Carolina teacher. He only started writing poetry during his last ten years of teaching. The poem "Turning of the Mind" is dedicated to the family of Dottie Batten, who has been suffering from and being treated for Alzheimer's disease. She is now in the advanced stage of this disease requiring around-the-clock care. She has a wonderful, caring family and a day nurse who manages her care. Mr. McKinney was inspired to compose this poem by observations made while working in the Batten's house over a period of three years.

Ordinary Day

I turn to wash my hands and stop to see hatred in your eyes
It seems my beating heart is what you despise
Your eyes are green like grass, yet black as your soul
It is clear to me that I'm not in control

The barrier, the line, and all hope breaks
I can't look away, I don't have what it takes
First sign of weakness is the itch in my eye
If I were to blink, I would surely die

The room dims black, it's just you and me
Your face is morphing, you change what I see
You are now a monster I haven't seen before
I sense that what's within you wants to start a war

My courage is gone, all my rights are wrong
What am I to do, you are far too strong
You take two steps forward and one step back
You can't wait to see how I will react

You seem to have had your fun, you release my mind
You release your ice-cold grip as if you're all too kind
The haze begins to fade and I begin to see clearer
And that is when I stop looking in the mirror

Laurie Luckritz

On a Cold Winter Day

On a cold winter day
Most would rather stay inside
Wrapped up in a warm blanket
Near the fireplace.

The sun shines bright
Through a big picture window.
Put on your sunglasses, to protect your eyes,
From the bright sunlight!

Oh, bright shining star,
You shine so bright
On a fresh blanket of snow
That is so white.

You put smiles on faces
When you shine so bright!
You lift spirits up
In addition, make the day go just right.

Oh happy day when the sun shines on a cold winter day.

Debra L. Bender

Wash Me Away

Wash me away…let me just breathe
Don't bring no questions to this weary mind; keep silent
Even if you hear the echoes of the night calling out
Don't just stare instead be about something
Spread your wings and fly away
Knowing it's okay to dream of a better tomorrow
But! Do be careful of the stepping stones
Some may be good…unsure of which ones
While stepping on the wrong one
Can be dangerous
Sending us straight to the cages of hell
When we belong up above with
God and His angels of love
Wash me away…just let me breathe…let me listen
Don't sit just counting the secrets of the untold stories,
of the untold lies
Instead embrace them into your lives
Knowing this is indeed
A beginning of something new; not the beginning of the end
For our salvation
Wash me away but don't say anything
Try not to pick nor point
For we all have flaws within us that shape our reality of life
Better yet we all have strength in us that can shape who we become
We don't have to stay stuck
In this past of time anymore
With the uncertainty of our flaming bush
If you see the tears that start
Do the right thing and just walk on by
But as soon as you start to take notice
The tears aren't water instead becoming the flesh of the heart
That is when it's time to do the wrong thing
And be a friend to the one in need
And don't just wash me away into the shadows

Corinne E. Brown

My name is Corinne E. Brown, born 1988 in the Bronx in New York. I currently still live in the Bronx with my grandma. I have also had one of my poems published through the World Poetry Movement back in January of 2012. I have been writing poetry since I was in grade school and through the love and support of my grandma, sisters and friends, I have decided to pursue having my voice heard by my poetry. I first started writing poetry through classwork and as time went on I was writing for fun. Then as I grew older, it became a way for me to express myself and now I am happy to be able to have the opportunity to share part of my life with others. When I am not writing poetry I attend church and help out my community.

Eternal Love!

I love you, the same
as you love me,
and when we deport,
your love stays with me.
Through the spirit of ether
I receive your love and give you back
the same for eternity.

This journey of life
here and now
on the planet Earth
it is for some time
then goes away
where it begins.

Shall we meet again
here and know?
When we understand what
always was and always will be
you and me—

the message of love.

Helen Blake

VFW Sky Pilot and Chaplain

My days as a chaplain, honored and performance at grave sights
Watched as many of my buddies were put to rest.
The wind whipped flags forever proudly flying
And many who have trod on foreign soil so defend it.
It's now given to the bereft family, life to "Old Glory," by request;
Now their loved ones are gone to supreme commander and all alone
They remain in silence at the grave sight, without a moan.
All their friends have silently departed, only a few abide,
The chaplain remains to give a helping hand, to console and pray;
His work is ever endless with funerals day to day.

Now the dear price that our buddies paid to fortify the world.
They are forgotten patriots, no banners to unfurl,
Then there comes a day of recognition, remembering them not;
They have all proudly served their country, and their honor forgot.
Every day I pray to God to guide my footsteps, lead me not astray,
Have concern for others and their needs daily, I pray.
I heard the voice of Jesus Christ, it came to me one day
In a tone sweet and calm, and I heard it say,
Carry on as Veteran's of Foreign War chaplain, I'll always care,
Remember you're serving your comrades, by your side I'll be there.

Pete "Wahoo" Preston

Pete "Wahoo" Preston was born in Horton, WY, August 1916. He started in Friendly Indians, then Scouting, and Eagle Scout advanced to Scoutmaster, Camp Director of Camp Kooi. Four years. Civilian Conservation Corps, U.S. Army three years, U.S. Navy thirty years. Retired Chief Petty Officer with 19,972 flying hours, fifty-seven combat missions. "Wahoo's" poetry has become loveable, treacherous, humorous and Godly. As nature generates its own aura, atmosphere, or magnetism, "Wahoo's" aura is in poetry's play of emotions, passions and feelings of metrical rhyming. "From His Crude Teepee," "He Saluted me," "The Scout of the Bygone Days." God's poetry, for we are God's workmanship, created in Christ Jesus to do good works, which God prepared in advance for us to do. Ephesians 2:10

The Truth

I am lost, and am being tossed around in a storm,
And nothing shows signs of being of the norm
Everything seems to be a little twisted.
And all my attempts to get out are being resisted
I'm lost in this controversy, because I've learned
the truth.
Making mostly everything a lie that I familiarized
myself with as a youth
The fiendish thing about the miseducation is that
it was premeditated
Giving me and my people a fools paradise
when we never were emancipated
So what do those of us do, who have come into
this realization?
We teach the truth to our kids and the ignorant
alike, in hopes that we can become a strong
and efficient nation.
So come out Black Man, the diagnosis has been made
No longer do we have to put up with the
Fiends' escapades.
Come out Black Man and be lost no more
True knowledge of self has opened up a sky
In which you choose how high to soar.

Marcus Gleaton

I've learned much over my thirty-eight years of life, and poetry has helped me to be able to express what I feel out loud. I have three daughters, Amber, Taylor and Arlalyjia, who inspire me to do my best, so this poem is for them. I want them to know that knowledge is the key, and that most limitations are self-imposed. Shoot for the stars, girls, that way even if you miss, you'll be amongst them.

Daddy Said This Day Would Come

Daddy said this day would come
I'm not ready to say goodbye
Tried to be strong Daddy
I can't help it if I cry
Oh God why?
I look up to the sky
Daddy said this day would come
I'm not ready to say goodbye
Life never will be the same
No calls about the game
Tears fall like rain
Heartaches walking down memory lane
Daddy said this day would come
I'm not ready to say goodbye
Lost without you is true
Momma loves you
What do we do?
We don't have a clue
Now so blue

Peggy Sue Lacroix

Would Anyone Care

If I were to die
Would one miss the happiness,
The joy and laughter
I gave off every moment?
Would the one I loved cry and show emotion
Or would I just fade away while he loves another?
If I were to leave
Would anyone follow
And stay with me till I parish
Or would I spend my time in darkness
Till the light shows me truth?
If I were to die
Would anyone care?

Cheyenne R. Angelo

A Teary Day

Up and around again,
I show a mad frown
Instead of a glad grin.
Back again before
Yesterday had to begin,
A teary day is right in front
Of me as I express
My sorry emotion of tears
So clear to see.

That particular day
Of work didn't go well.
More of my own frustration
Didn't waste any hesitation
On making me picture
Myself locked in a dark place.
Accompanied with a sad face,
I knew if I didn't try
To regain a never-quit warrior face,
All of the internal and external fears I face
Will forever give me a teary day.

If I did just look at failure
As a sad way of envisioning
A bleak future,
Then a teary day
Will always be in my way
Even after I pray.

Daniel Brett Johnson

Worn

The softness of your touch has now come to wither
The sweet taste of your kiss has now become bitter
Every word you have said is now empty and hollow
Now I am left in my sorrow, forever to wallow

Every kiss, every touch that steals breath from my chest
Is now worthless, but keeps me unable to rest
Every word that could warm me through most brutal winter
Were lies, leaving my heart the harshest of splinters

Entrapped and enchanted, you made my heart feel
That someone who cared for it now became real
With your touch you were able to lie and to fool me
To believe in this love which is never to be

Kirby Harrell

Vitality

Rise at dawn then rest at dusk,
today will leave as quick as it came.
Yesterday's routine summons you once more,
and your life remains mundane.
Suppressed by forceful ropes,
gladly tightened by humanity.
Only he who holds freedom's blade,
can escape this profanity.

Set forth to your hearts desire,
drifting upon gentle waves at sea.
To the peak of the highest mountain,
or on the sand beneath a palm tree.
Perhaps standing deserted in a field,
to loudly holler at the moon.
Or purely settling in the tall grass,
on a warm evening in June.

An exotic spirit is trapped inside,
with a lingering hunger to roam.
T'is not satisfied with your ambiance.
And this place you call "home".
Rise at dawn then rest at dusk,
today will leave as quick as it came.
Your body hides the burning desire
of its free spirit that has no shame.

Giovanna Iaffaldano

Direttore Aria

There's something about performing for hours on end,
Just to hear your music from around the bend.
Practicing practicing, it brings your heart's amend...
When that moment comes to you, perfection, it doesn't have to end.

When you least expect it, when your ear listens dull,
The sound comes full force again; hands, eyes and mind working together.
That realization that that sound's coming from you.
And all you do is stare.

To practice for ten hours, just to play a three minute song,
That's why I play music, and it turns out, I've known this all along.

You see? That space between each note?
Just as important as the notes themselves.
There lies nuance and passion, cadence and love.
This is what, and why, I share.

That space separates all the musicians' ideas.
Crafting the story he writes with each bow.
Like a poem: a thing in history, a staple of forever,
With all the markings, noting allemandes and fortissimos!

Whether in an orchestra, band, or symphony,
Or just playing for someone dear,
I wish for with my music, it would change just one person's life,
And I found that one person . . . is already here.

Patrick Hansen

Growing up in performing arts, music is what pulled me through mourning my parents' deaths. Their memories are irreplaceable, much like a cello on my chest, a violin on my cheek, or a piano under my hands.

Centennial Star Tribute

A budding nation
Purity of thought surrounds
The bright fire within

Yellow rays are born
Unfold like the rising sun
Spreading love and hope

Desiring freedom
Fire and tempers bloom to fight
One against another

Working together
Melding true freedom throughout
Built a new nation

Elaine Carroll Kelley

My inspiration was the beauty of the Centennial Star Hybrid Tea Rose. This rose allowed the privilege of watching a nation being built by its mesmerizing beauty. Its purity and fire laced with love unfolded each day reminding me our country was built by our brave forefathers day by day. My poem is to honor all Americans who continue to work together to keep our nation strong. Poetry has helped me through the rough times in my life. Thank you Great Poets Across America for honoring me and giving me the opportunity to share my poem.

Oblivion

I am in oblivion I talk I yell I scream but no one seems to hear me
I run I jump I fly but what am I
Last I remember I was lying on the ground war raging all around
I see crow flying all around while I lay there on the ground
There's a light nearby is that my life passing by

Cheyenne Jarman

My Apprentice Lily

Once she was alone and barely alive.
Her sister was taken from her arms.
Holding onto the hope her kin would survive,
She crawls away without raising an alarm.
Bleeding on the side of the road.
Eyes filled with pain and sadness, she begins to cry.
If death was buying her life, it would be sold.
On the brink of death, she is saved by a samurai.
Using ancient magic, her wounds healed faster.
The will was strong, but her plan was bold.
Bowing before him, she called him master.
Learning lessons from the demon with a soul,
Sword vs. sword, her style of sword play was unique.
Looking for her sister, she was on a quest.
Her master told her to never accept defeat.
Out of all his apprentices, she was the best.
Finding her sister as her story unfolds.
Fifty vs her? The odds are quite silly.
But protecting her sister is her only goal.
Go get them, girl! That is my apprentice Lily!

Brandon Oliver

Two Lovers

Drops of rain tapping on my window pane
Emotions swirling in stride
Lovers lose track of time
Piano pings a chord
Music of sweet accord
Dancing alongside you
Intricately combined through heart and soul
A lover's touch well-known
A whisper in melody
A grasp of serenity
Dancing harmoniously
As to be one eternally
Lovers gently kiss
Lips pressed together in bliss
The music plays
As two become one this day
One look of ease
Love has been released
Pouring out of control
Into their hearts as foretold
Dancing alongside you
Intricately combined through heart and soul
A lovers touch well-known
A kiss goodnight
We'll see each in mornings sunrise
I love you
Adieu, adieu

Christina Potts

Lost Perspective

I used to want your eyes,
so that I may see into the souls of others.
But the end of days has yet to come
and I could not bear to steal from God.
I'll find an ending, somehow,
to this petty life of mine,
A beginning for an unblemished heart.

I may be denied your eyes
But I shall receive one last look.

Elizabeth Buck

That's Just Life

Life is a steep hill.
It has its ups and downs.
Sometimes you stumble,
Sometimes you fall.
But that's just life.

Sometimes you fall down,
and feel as though you can't go on.
Pick yourself up and try again.
Life is a steep hill,
and that teaches us to be strong and carry on.

Because that's just life.

Marie-Josee Larouche

For as long as I can remember I have had a passion for writing poems. It has always been my dream to get published. It is a great honor to have been chosen to have my world published, and I couldn't be any happier than I am now.

Three Words

Hanging by three words
The hint was bold
He turned around
Meeting me nose to nose
We had this moment
Somehow perfect at best
I whispered "I love you"
As I felt the heat of his chest
My hands pressed hard
Pushing away
Trying to hide
Trying to think of what to say
He removed my hands
That covered my face
Looking at me deeply
Pulling me into his embrace
He lifted my chin
Looked me straight in my eyes
Feeling a tear roll down my cheek
I suddenly realized
He was pulling me closer
Slowly kneeling down
I felt our lips meet
Then I couldn't hear a sound
I felt sparks of insanity
My whole body went numb
I couldn't believe it
I found him, the one.

Kaylee Holloway

Poetry has inspired me in many ways. It's given me the chance to share my dreams and fantasies with others, and possibly inspire them as well. Poetry lets me express myself more than anything else could. It's the easiest way for me to show my real emotions and actually put them in words. I thank God every day for giving me this wonderful gift.

Perfect Blossom

There is nothing so beautiful as to die on a field of green.
A life lived too long is one of mourning and pain.
But sweet suffering is at last as calm as a gentle stream.
A calm like no other, none that I can name.
Beyond the shades of red, I see my beloved, almost like a dream.
I see her face so warm and sweet, and the wilderness around me seems so tame.
I call to her in one final roar, as off she goes and,
then the sound of battle fires again, and I remember our fight and fame.
The bodies fall down all around me, I see my men shot and
with my sword in my bloody hand I dare not take this final shame.
I notice my reflection and the blade's red gleam
I'll die with honor for our family and our name.

My final moments are flickering away like the cherry blossoms on the air.
It can sometimes take a lifetime to find the perfect flower,
but I can see them all floating now, I can see you standing there,
right under that precious tree, the wind fanning your precious hair
I focus only on your beauty, on all the simple power
of the cherry blossoms flying, it gives me more love than I can bear.

Even as I close my eyes, I can never recreate the time that flies.
Laying on the field of green, gazing up at the sky serene.
I weep my final tear, for I know you will soon be near.
Now I'll meet my death, but with my last breath
I'll sing to you my love, that I'll see your face
in another place, high up above,
where the perfect blossoms fly.

George Kliamenakis

This poem was inspired by and based off Katsumoto, from the film The Last Samurai (2003). *I actually felt this man's pain and loneliness towards the end of his death. To know love so vividly and passionately and then to have it torn away from you must be the worst hell imaginable. Today's love is cruel, one-sided and often mistaken for lust, but what he had in the movie was probably the most real and beautiful rendition of love I have ever seen.*

Drunk in Love

With one red rose in hand I dance
along the beach to the rhythm of the
sea intoxicated by your love as my
soul feels the fire of our last
passionate kiss...I stumble along
the sea shore in my drunken dance
as moonshine and starshine seduce
me...In the morning I awake
holding one red rose in hand as
the sea washes over me...

William Cagliostro

I pray my writings make the world a better place. That is why I created Windy Island Nights inspirational greeting cards and books. I give my cards away out of love and I pray others give out of love to Florida Baptist Children's Homes of Lakeland, FL because they care for orphans. I have great love and compassion for orphans, mentally ill, homeless, handicapped, prostitutes, elderly, animals and all that lives, hurts and suffers. I also created No Petroleum Vehicle Charity to manufacture affordable, safe, planet friendly vehicles out of love in an effort to end greed.

God Given Rights

My ancestors lived here in the hills and the plains, with not a sound for miles, not even the trains. They survived cold winters off the game and the grain. You shall slap your mouth if you dare to call the people lame. They signed the declaration that led us to our God given rights, even though they were well aware it could have caused many fights. I send out a salute to those who bled in the fields, with not one thought to stop or to yield. They threw up their arms and died like men, and God didn't claim it as one of their sins. Hopeless dreams, sleepless nights, please don't take away another one of my God given rights!

Briar Von Ohlen

Forgotten

The world turns a blind eye
As we lose the true color of the sky
Searching for simple pleasures in life
While nature is now paying the price
Nature has always been
Now it's about to end

Losing our individuality to similarity
Life becomes a pattern of movement
Only a concern for self-improvement

The sound of buzzing bumble bees
Birds flying among the tranquil trees
All forgotten to paying tax fees

Reality is insanity
Confused with what really we need
With things we want to succeed

Say goodbye to the open range
Until the world is willing to change

Mariah Oetken

Fallen Soldier

Fallen soldier all alone, fallen soldier far from home.
Trickling down his face a tear forgetting how it feels to fear.
Death and all its fate and glory now it's here no need to fear he's one they will all forget.
Now breathing's just a waste of breath and living's just a waste of death as he searches for this new address, a brand new home free of loneliness.
Lying motionless on the ground, the battle raging all around.
For now he's is not alone this fallen soldier has found his new home.
No unwanted tears, no wounded peers.
It is forever now we sit and wait to see his sweet loving face.
It's your time no my dearly beloved soldier, take your stand; your mission is now complete. Forever may you rest in peace.

Nikki Woods

The Moon

When you go to the moon,
I hope I'll see you soon.
Say it isn't so,
I bet you'll see its glow.
Take pictures for me,
And bring me the key.
I wish I could go with you,
Imagine all the stuff we would do,
I'll give you a clue.
We could say "hi" to a crater,
What would be greater.
We could see our flag,
To see if it wags.

Lauryn Santos

Jesus

Jesus, You are my strong Savior
My hiding place in time of need
I stand here tonight as a rapper
But this is not who I am
I am Your servant and You are my lead

You see,
I'm here to tell You about Christ's story
But ultimately give Him glory
Because if I don't
This song will just be boring

Christ died to give us life
He died because He loved us
To rescue us from a life of strife
You see Christ forgave us
And did everything He promised

He saved us from our sins
And broke every chain we held within
He pulled us from the brink of death
And gave us eternal breath

We need to thank Him
And praise Him for all He's done
Because without Him we are all undone

Our Savior is high above all names
And we should not be ashamed
For He alone is with us
And forever victorious

So as I finish this song
Know that when you are weak
Christ is strong
And in Him we belong

Tiffany Amber Swingle

I am Tiffany Swingle and I am currently nineteen years old. I am deeply inspired by what my Savior Jesus Christ has done for me on the cross. I find joy in sharing the Gospel with others and so in my poem I wanted to do just that! Poetry is a way I can express myself through words and be creative. I'm very thankful and blessed to have been given the opportunity to share this beautiful gift God has graciously given to me with the world.

Breaking My Glass Mask

My mask is slowly breaking
upon my unseen face.
No one has seen the true me,
and now I'm scared
they will see me cry.
My tears will fall, all at once.
My smile has already begun to fade.
With my mask of glass that's slowly breaking
I hear the cricking and the cracking;
it's slowly breaking apart.
My mask of glass is slowly breaking.
It's letting me be me
so everyone will know who I really am.
I want them to know I'm not some fake going
along with the crowd.
My tears are real, my laugh is real, my smile is real.
Although I can't quite say I'm me,
I am different.
I know I will cry and frown and put a new mask on,
but I will always know there is someone out there
who can make me smile, make me laugh, and break
my brand new mask.

Emily Stallman

Untitled

c
r
y
s
t
a
l
tear drops
clinking sharp notes
of and of and
t g s h
r i w a
u v a n
e i y g
* n i i
a g n n
b * g g
s r * *
o e t b
l s o y
u t * *
t i c a
i t a *
o u d t
n t e h
I n r
o c e
n e a
d

Donna Anair King

My Hubby

You're always there
No matter where you are
I know you're my man for years now
Even when the chips are down
You're always around
When we made love it was familiar
And I remembered why we became one together
Just wanted to say it one more time...
You're still the one, my number one,
The only one for me....
I think thirty-five years total should buy
Me at least fifty years more
On our totem pole of life, love, and happiness
I love you, my number one

Debra Rogers

I was inspired by the love and devotion of my husband. He has been there through good and bad times and has never let me down. Just a little note of thanks, Frank. Love Always, Debra

Entity

"Nothing is real," that's what it told me,
but that can't be true, life's all around me.
It continued on, explaining sadly.
To my surprise, I'm understanding.
I look around me and see not the world,
but fields of lost chaos, layered in lies.
The trees do not grow, they simply rise,
and rivers don't flow, "how silly" it sighs.
The sky isn't blue, nor oceans deep.
Even when singing we make not a peep.
I look to the stars, and realize the truth.
Only what dies, lives as if alive.
It turned to the west and faded away,
but before it was gone it wanted to say.
"Nothing is real, and nothing can stay."

Jesse Vincent Malysz

My Shadow

The smile, the face, the radiant eyes,
I lie awake and think of you and I.
The heart, the soul, the everlasting love,
My eyes shoot open when I think of you.
Three words I say, seem to take your breath away.
But four words to say, would jolt you in my arms immediately.
But before these four words softly flow from my lips.
I want to tell you this.
You are my light, my life, my soul, my might.
No one could ever take the place you, out of my sight.
No one could...
No one would...
I want to be with you more than you could ever imagine,
Until these next few words become a new age sin.
I'll love you, forever and always.
You are my love, my shadow, my only one.
So will you marry me?
And be with me through anything and everything?

Justin Mitchell

Against the Crowd

Standing alone...
can seem the worst
with a faded smile,
shadowed eyes,
and tears that burst.

But, standing alone...
will test our strength.

Jordan Stickle

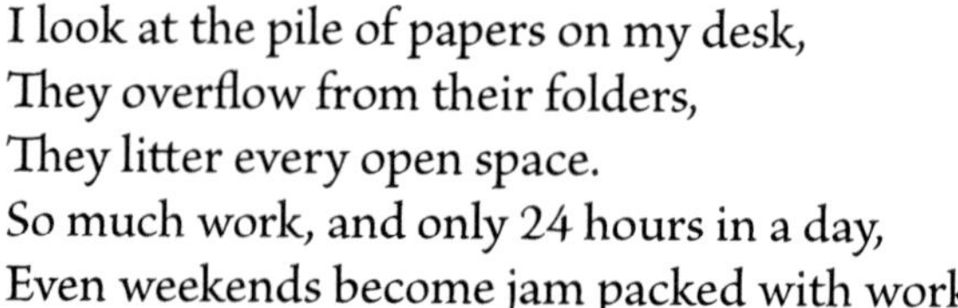

Life of an AP Student

I look at the pile of papers on my desk,
They overflow from their folders,
They litter every open space.
So much work, and only 24 hours in a day,
Even weekends become jam packed with work.
Never a free moment in sight.
Papers need to be written,
Tests need to be studied for,
Worksheets need completion.
No break is in sight.
An unopened book rests near it all,
Its pages untouched and crisp.
Yet its contemporary, the textbook, is battered and open,
Note paper creeping over the book's edge.
Pencil's lead smudging. Pen ink bleeding.
As the school year continues — the work does also.
No time for writer's cramp to heal.
Sleepless nights spent working on it all.
One assignment blurs into the next:
It all needs to be done.
Teachers keep the load coming,
As if we only take that class.
No relaxation on the horizon.
As the year comes to a close,
Review work continues on top other assignments.
Finally final exams have arrived,
They signal the end of all the work;
Until summer assignments are handed out,
Even during the two months off, we work nonstop.
Before we know it, school is back.
It's a constant pattern of study, work, repeat,
A never ending cycle of papers,
Littering cluttered desktops: the life of an AP student.

Jennifer Plouffe

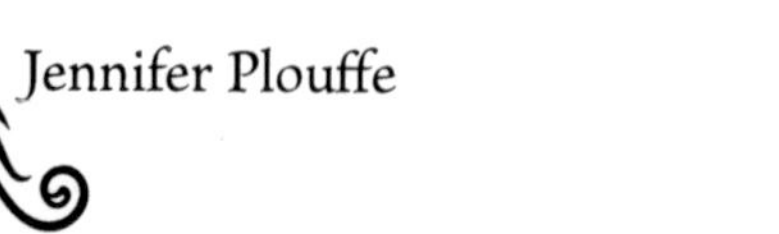

Coming Home: The Gift

The box sat for years
In Gran's closet next to shoes

The remains of a tortured soul
No sun or breeze upon a face

A life no longer lived but gone
Just ash in tin and cardboard

Placed there then forgotten by family
No more friends to stop by and question

Drawn out illness
Forcing Heaven's journey

Years later a forgotten child
Receives a paper bag

Its contents the remains
Her father who ran out on her

Causing years of terrible pain
Had finally found his true home

An urn she now placed him in
Brown and trimmed with gold

It sits upon her shelf each day
Reminding her she is no longer alone

Mary Tuohy

As a member of the Farmingdale Writer's Group and the Farmingdale Poetry Group in Long Island, NY, I am able to share my love for poetry. I also enjoy writing stories and hope to write novels as well. Recently I had a poem titled "A Rose in Bloom" published by the World Poetry Movement, and it is included in their anthology entitled Stars in Our Hearts: Hope. *A second poem "My Champion" is to be published in an anthology by them in May 2012. Another recent accomplishment is knowing two more poems "Betrayed" and "The To Do List" will be published very soon in a local anthology entitled* Whispers and Shouts, *a book of poems by Long Island women about women's issues. It is a great honor to have my work included in this publication.*

Do Not Fear

When life flows in like a crashing wave,
And you feel like all hope is lost, and you're about to cave,
Have faith, you're strong enough to make it through,
It's never too late to start again, brand new.
When you find yourself stranded in the valley of doubt,
And you feel like there will never be a way out,
Keep going, until you see that ray of light
That can brighten the darkest of nights.
Life is the most beautiful gift given,
You have a purpose here,
Never feel that you are forbidden
From happiness,
You deserve the best.
Never,
Ever,
Settle for anything less.
True beauty
Is not found in physical features
No, it goes much deeper,
To the very depths of your heart,
And even if it's breaking apart,
Do not fear,
These things will make you strong
The pain will not stay, soon it will be gone,
And you will realize, there was no need to worry,
All along.

Amanda Stirling

Another Cloud

You can't control these things
these things you know
this I'm saying to myself
when the bottle is empty
it hits me

twisted acceptance enrolls me
I've never felt so free
tomorrow I'll see flight
another cloud will surely pass

there's a light for me
over there on the other side
so I wait and wait
nothing can break my stride
temptation was fun in the past
but it never took me anywhere too fast

I see devil's playing
in your fields
why do you question all the warnings?
I'll be miles away
when they finally get you
and turn you into waste

think I'll take the high road
the low one has got me down

Nate Blesse

Glass Heart

My hear is made of glass,
Glass that can be easily broken
I have a broken glass heart

Please be kind to my glass heart, and I will be kind to yours
Don't make my glass heart shatter
As others have done so many time before

Be different than the rest who hurt me
Because I love you, I want you to be different
Are you different, will you be careful with my glass heart?

Please treasure my glass heart
I've always tried my best to be careful with your glass heart
So please treasure and love this glass heart

My glass heart is broken
I don't want to be forever broken
Please put me back together again

I have a broken glass heart
Put it back together
Please put me back together with your love

Susanna Thurston

Lonely Serenata

Everything is Love
Forgotten winter and cold nights
Identity lost its mirror
I belong to now not tomorrow
Between snow and sun
Solitude!
Forgotten are yesterday's shadows
And twilight nights
Forgotten dreams are suddenly
Lights without depth
So very transparent like
The late blooming rose
I have found my wings
Forgotten are the thorns
Of the cactus
Forgotten are the drunken eyes and rage
I have been reborn like the mustard seed
From the red earth
I want to touch fire
As I have already touched oblivion
I have laid with dead cold corpses
I look for the eternal wind
And devouring calmness of the noble night.

Linda E. Daggett

God Is Never Gone

Though my heart is stricken with despair
though I am entangled in the world's snare
God is never gone
never will say to me "Hold on"

My Lord will never leave me nor forsake me
as he promises in Hebrews thirteen
God is never gone
never will he say to me "Be gone"

I am with the Lord Jesus Christ
Oh, how His is more than sufficed
because He took my punishment on the cross
so I wouldn't be in chaos

Under all of this
I can have bliss
because
God is never gone
now I can see him in the dawn

Jordan Wiese

Oak Tree

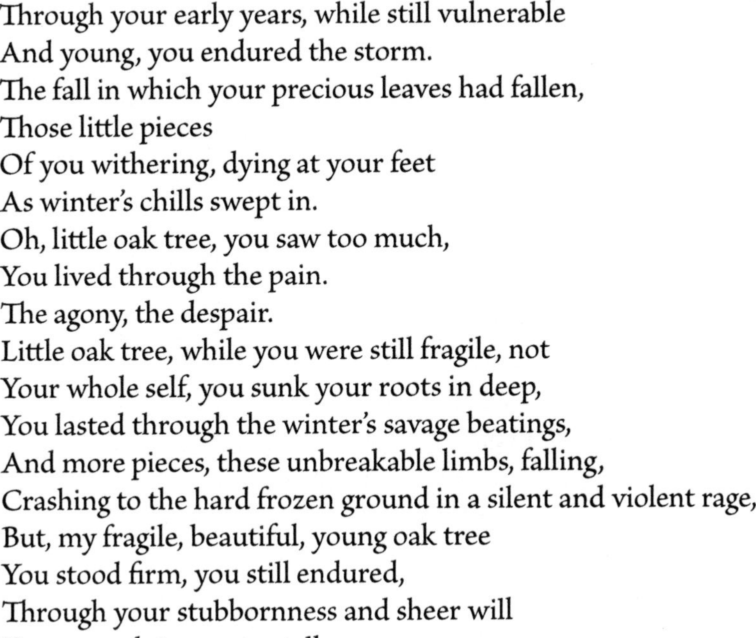

Through your early years, while still vulnerable
And young, you endured the storm.
The fall in which your precious leaves had fallen,
Those little pieces
Of you withering, dying at your feet
As winter's chills swept in.
Oh, little oak tree, you saw too much,
You lived through the pain.
The agony, the despair.
Little oak tree, while you were still fragile, not
Your whole self, you sunk your roots in deep,
You lasted through the winter's savage beatings,
And more pieces, these unbreakable limbs, falling,
Crashing to the hard frozen ground in a silent and violent rage,
But, my fragile, beautiful, young oak tree
You stood firm, you still endured,
Through your stubbornness and sheer will
You, my oak tree, grew tall.

As the spring came, the harsh winds blown
Away, you sprouted new branches, new graceful limbs
That took hold of your newly green budding leaves.
And now, oak tree, no longer young as you were,
Another winter is coming.
Another piece, just newly fallen...
But, my gorgeous enduring oak,
You will survive.
For just as the storm of your youth, this is the same.
And as that young fragile sapling you stood tall, you
Took the brunt of winter's violent beatings,
And alive and well as you are now, my oak,
I know that once again you will stand your ground, keep
Those roots dug in deep, my oak,
And through this one last brutal winter,
You will survive.

Amber E. Herberg

On the Spectrum

Over seven billion of us swim this earthen sea.
For at least one in ninety a current pushes us differently.
The Autism spectrum is their eddy to be.
Some claim a pill will one day make it all go away.
Will not work that way as it came combined in our DNA.
Sometimes a crowded room can be a daunting task.
Must step back, take a deep breath to avoid reaching critical mass.
At times you would think I lack total empathy. Before you judge quickly
You have to see it doesn't flow from me naturally.
You may see a blank stare, but trust implicitly I do care.

Class president, football hero, class clown, prom king, may or may not be.
Perhaps regrets for things I may have done inappropriately.
Maybe I could go back and do them differently.
Will I be able to live the life of what is called neurotypically.
Perhaps a greater power does not want it to be.

Robert Stuart

so what do you want then?

perfect
you called me perfect
no, you called me more than that
you said i was everything
you'd ever dreamed of
even better than that actually
and that every day i got even better
that you couldn't believe
how happy i made you
and how perfect i was
i did everything i could
to get better
to be as perfect as possible
to make sure that opinion didn't change
and to keep it going
but you did leave me
you stopped loving me
and you say it's not my fault
but if i was so perfect
what could have possibly
made you stop loving me
what is so much more enticing
than something so much better than perfect
that it could take you away
if I was everything you could ever want
even more than that
then why don't you want me anymore
what more do you want?

Krystal Ann Schilling

Believe

The lonely child standing by herself
The quiet one who has dolls on her shelf
No one wants to be friends with her
They hear she's different, even though they aren't sure
Her big eyes are always filled with tears
From being alone all these years
She has no hope, she has no mom or dad
And as the days pass she's always so sad
She remembers the dark and the fear
But her parents were near
So she falls asleep in the back of the car
But she didn't know that those men had been to the bar
She felt the smash, the terrifying screech of metal
As her dad tries to control the car's spinning with the brake pedal
But it's no use, the car crashes
Her parents fly forward and her head bashes
She slips into the dark, just a child
She wakes up to a light, the aches only mild
The nurse tells her, her parents are dead
She doesn't understand this fear and dread
She has no reason to feel this way
But she does, every day
One day, she meets another girl
Who has the same big eyes where emotions whirl
She lost her parents to a crash too
And now everyday she's blue
The girls talk, only seven now, so young
Sharing secrets, comparing where their lives went wrong
But now they have each other, best friends
They made it through what they thought was the end
They finally see a new light
So shiny, yellow and bright
They hold each other's hands and smile

They know they haven't felt this in a while
And now they finally believe

Ashley Stephens

Poetry is my everything. I would not have pursued it if I had not had the constant support from my family and friends. This is for my dad, mom, and little brother, as well as my close friends—Katie Bass, Brian Noe and all of you! Thank you so much for all your love and support.

Dreaming Is Reality

Oh how I dream of sleep but
when I sleep the dreams make me weep.

I may not remember what the reason was for this commotion,
yet I still feel the painful emotion
that drags me down to the ground just to be kicked around.

As I begin to rain
and release all this pain
that I have been building up making me go insane,
I scream to the sky...

Why!?

What have I done to deserve this?
I was but an angel of bliss.

Smiling all day and night,
seeing the sun even in spite
of all the darkness that surrounds me.

All I shall do is fly
high in the sky screaming...

Why!?

As I begin to soar
away from my problems once more,

the obscurity of my reality
slices through my core.
Flying exists no more...

Falling hurts the most
when you begin to see your ghost.
Screaming in distress...

Why!?

Retentions flash in my soul
while the rubicund gale causes me to roll
deep into the marines floor.

My lungs begin to shrink
as I begin to sink,
deeper and deeper into unconsciousness.

Looking up
at the last bit of light
in my life
pondering

Why!?

Jessica McFadden

I am a junior in high school. This is my third poem to be published. Acclaimed *was the first book which contains "Trash."* Stars in Our Hearts *is the second book which holds "Pallid Moon." Now* Great Poets Across America *with "Dreaming Is Reality." I am so thankful for all of the opportunities that you have given me. I love poetry and everything about it.*

Suicidal

All warmth is gone
Heart to ice
How wouldn't death be nice

I put the barrel
To my chest
Pull the trigger for my death
I missed my heart
I'm still alive
Another day that I survived
Kill me please.

I put the knife
To my wrist
Slide the blade with a hiss
I missed my vein
I'm still alive
Another day that I survived
Kill me please.

I put the rope
To my cheek
Then I think, what the heck
I missed my chance
I'm still alive
Another day that I survived
Never mind now.

I put the cloth
To my nose
Now relax; it's life I chose
Too late I realize
Death that looms
In the cloth were deadly fumes.

Cynthia Wallis

I Will Be Happy Today

I will be happy today, through the darkest moments, most painful times, come light, come dark, or brightest shine.

I am not a prisoner, I am not chained to my bed. I am only chained to all the things I allow to haunt me in my own head.

I will be happy today—the sky is blue or the sky is gray, come rain, come shine, come what awful may.

I can take deep breaths, I can feel my hands, I can walk to and fro with legs that help me fix my woes.

Truth be known, this is not our home, and we are never left alone. Though it seems this pain won't end, or this day is awful, our final day is set in stone.

For we do not walk this earth alone. We have gifts, precious and few, others who walk by our side and help to pull us through.

So today I have chosen to look for at least one good thing to keep me going, for which to be grateful and try my best not to be hateful.

For hateful brings a bigger debt, it takes us down to a deeper depth, a darker place, which darkens our heart's door and doesn't allow the sun to touch our face, to pull us through with its gentle healing warm embrace.

Yes, today I will find at least one good thing.

Mary Quintero

Winter Nights

Winter days, with stormy nights
Body frozen over, blood thick as ice
No view of survivors in my sight

All alone
Nothing but the fire that burns inside
All alone
Too weak to walk, too weak to cry

I've got no air left in my lungs
I can't shout out for help

I am dying now, cold and alone
On this cold winter night
There's no need to fight
There's nothing I can do, I guess it's just my time

They'll probably find my body in three weeks or so
I had no friends, I had no wife
No one will notice I've been missing all this time

I have nothing to look forward to
Nothing to decide
I can die right now, on this cold winter night

I've got no strength left, no will to survive
No one will miss me after I die

Geovanny Luna

I was born in East Los Angeles, CA in June, 1991. My father died when I was four and my mother raised three kids alone. She was working, going to school, and raising us. I used to hate the fact that she was always busy. It took me awhile to realize everything she did was for us. Mom, thank you. I discovered my skills for writing in school. Creative writing allowed me to express myself and my thoughts. Every now and then ideas just pop in my head and I write them down. I have started several books but never finished any. But little by little all my ideas are going down on paper. I will finish them and get them published.

Almost Gone, but Found

Suffocating, falling faster
Into the darkness. Catch me.

Falling slowly into the deep.
I can't feel you. Not even in my sleep.

The air is fading. I try to hold on.
Is my heart still beating?

Bring me out of this place.
Let me feel your breath on my face.

Pick me up and carry me out.
I scream, but I make no sound.

I hear your voice in the distance,
Coming closer with each footstep.

The one who loves me is finally here.
It's like the sun coming out of the clouds.

Almost gone, almost lost my life.
But you found me just in time.

Maggie Roig

First, I would like to thank God for giving me this amazing talent. Next, I want to thank my friends and family for their support and encouragement. Finally, I want to thank my friend/editor, Courtney Caruso, for helping me with this poem. Poetry is my life. I thank God for saving it.

The Road Ahead

Open vastness, the isolated stretch
of highway lies belly up before
vehicles barreling through.

Making head-way as horizon
meets earth at distances
unseeable to open minds.

While shrubbery stubbles the desert
land, clouds lazily play above
God's moveable mountains.

An endless, voided sky gapes
as an open doorway to Heaven.
God beckons His child to belief
through the hints of magnificence
strewn before our feet.

I starve to see His power displayed
before me. Every breath I feel
His divine spirit crackling with energy.
Surging with life, He envelops our
earth in beauty. Only created by
His hands.

My road still has length to be traveled
as time begins to play its part.

Desert scenery illuminates from
effect of the sun's now setting
departure.

Janine Naquin

Adam & Eve "The Forbidden Fruit"

The Bible tells a story of where life began
it's a story of a woman and her man
A story of how, lust and greed would play a part
and of a love that was, that never had a start
It's where the woman would be the one to blame
for every man's sin just the same
Her name was Eve and in time
would be the intended mother of mankind
Then there was Adam and her lover
and with a holy bond God brought them together
Then there was a serpent that came on down
and it was the woman that he found
He told her a story of what she was about
he made her wonder he made her doubt
He gave her hints, he gave her clues
he told her lies, he told her what to do
He told her what he wanted her to hear
never giving in, he had no fear
for it would be the woman who would shed a tear
He told her, "Take a bite, and it won't be long
and you will surely know right from wrong."
So she took a bite and gave it to her man
she told him what to do, she said, "You Can!"
but once he took a bite their problems began
It's because of a serpent why they would believe
that would cause them to sin to bring them to their knees
It's where greed and lust would be the cause of this crime
in taking what's yours and making it mine
It was a love to lust which turned them to hate
which led to their downfall and our fate
And all for a taste and a lust to partake
and the love of a God that they forsake

Marvin T. Trujillo

The Never-Ending War

Do you like tearing me apart,
you should stop if you know what's smart.
Could you leave me alone and let me live my life,
do you realize you're the one causing this strife?
You're putting family against family, friend against friend,
someone is going to turn up dead of this doesn't end.
You keep putting more people in danger each day,
quit ignoring me and listen to what I say.
Stop this nonsense and this fight,
it doesn't matter who was wrong or right.
I just want this to be over and done,
we'll consider this war never won.

Sabrina Ann Stone

Surface

Like a memory I have not lived, or a life I cannot recall....
Your eyes have captured that missing space.
And in the windows of your spaced-out gleam, I know it all.
Time and time again, through the phonaion and the footsteps,
this vision rises....
Your voice, echoing a history I cannot grasp, a predispositioned
certainty, lost in a cylindrical time frame as a mirror faces another,
somewhere unseen.
The reflection, ceaseless, as if an eternal labyrinth.
But those elite moments, in which our eyes meet . . . I find
you again.
Your touch revives those embedded towers,
brings them to the surface after the waves subside....
And there you are, gleaming into my eyes, once more.

Dianna Bandy

Real Me

Please don't judge me by my face
By my religion or my race
Please don't laugh at what I wear
Or how I look or do my hair
Please look a little deeper
Way down deep inside
And although you might not see it
I move a lot to hide
Behind my clothes a secret lies
Behind my smile I softly cry
Please listen to me
I will show you I'm insecure
Please try to be a friend to me
Show me that you care
Please just get to know me
And maybe you will see
That if you look deep enough
You will find the real me

Ted "TJ" Myers

Born in Port Perry, ON, to Ted and Lori in 1977, I was raised by my grandparents Robert and Gladys Burgess in Oshawa, ON. I started writing poetry in 1992 when I was sent to a group home. I am a recovering drug addict, and I write most of my poems about things I have experienced over the years, and the pain and suffering my heart has endured.

Loyal Hero

A fat little boy all alone
Sensed that no one cared
His heart broken, his spirit crushed
By criticism and unnecessary comments
Things soon get better, when he meets his loyal hero

Every day he impatiently waits to get off the bus
Because when he does he retrieves unconditional love
Yep. That's right. From his loyal hero
He soon begins to depend on seeing him...waiting patiently for the bus
His loyal hero soon becomes his only friend
His only friend became his only companion

Then one day he looks out the bus to see no one waiting patiently
He looks around and calls his name
But finds not one thing
Once again his heart is broken, his spirit crushed
He knows his loyal hero has left him all alone

Every day goes by so slowly
Without his friends greetings
But soon his dad proves his loyalty
Later his dad becomes his loyal hero
Then his hero becomes his friend
Until the day his dad leaves his side

Later in life he spends his days helping those in need
Bring hope and joy into the lives of many who struggle
He knows/understands the feelings of loneliness and despair
He soon becomes a loyal hero to many
Some times without even knowing it
He has dedicated his life to God first
Family/friends second
And those in need third

His past experiences...
His love of God...
His loyal heroes...
Taught him everything he knows now

Elisabeth George

Forevermore

Sights unseen
laughter unlaughed
Smiles unsmiled
and tears not shed
as you lay in your
eternal bed
Flowers unbloomed as
life took you way too soon
the brightness of the
sun no more
insanity the only door
for this has shaken
me to the core
'tis you are gone
Forevermore
Forevermore
From my arms you
are forever tore!

Tonya Allen Stone

I am a proud army brat who grew into a woman who has been down many roads and seen many things. Through it all, I believe in God and we will all be together one day. This poem is in memory of my sweet Sara Jade, you were an angel long before you left this earth, and to my Justin and Summer, always believe there is truth and love out there, but don't be deceived—there are also lies and hate that lurk in the shadows! Butterfly and Eskimo kisses! Sara my daughter—you will have justice!

Filched from Fatal Fate

In the dead of night while I sat writing notes from a bed on the veranda
With my parents and siblings fast asleep in the house
I was distracted by a muffled noise
On looking around I saw nothing untoward, and so continued writing
However, I couldn't shake off a sense of foreboding
And so uttered a short prayer against any hidden danger
All of a sudden, the cute little kitty which lay on my bed
Stood up hissing, arching its back with its tail up and hair on end
I turned round to see and froze—
There right behind me, just a few inches away from my thighs
Was a black, speckled and deadly poisonous krait!
I moved my thighs quietly, inch by inch towards the edge of the bed
On reaching the edge I leapt forward and escaped
Almost simultaneously the snake too leapt and went under the bed and was killed

Solomon G. Gunapalan

Dear Boy

Can I have the privilege to take care of your heart
Do I have the ability to keep you from falling apart
Could I hold you close and listen to your eyes for just a second
Could I kiss your lips, and live my dreams I have neglected

Can we lay and watch the stars as the world spins 'round
Can we dance among the clouds without making a sound
Could we sail across the skies on the milky way
Could we walk on water on a warm summer day

Could we fly over the tree tops without a care
Could we close our eyes, and imagine we are anywhere
Can I steal you a way, for just a little while
Can I kiss your nose just to see you smile

Can we achieve the impossible when we are together
Can we find the truth in forever
Could we fall asleep on a rose, under a pedal
Could we runaway and get lost in a beautiful meadow

Dear Boy,
Could we forget about reality, and just live out our dreams
Believe in our fantasy, no matter how crazy it seems
Could we believe the unbelievable, and do the undone
Could we fight a war that has never been won

Could I teach you how to love, if you could just teach me
The sky is the limit, there is so much we could be
Anything is possible when I am with you
You have opened my eyes to something real
And something true

Olivia Ferguson

I am so grateful to be able to have one of my poems published in celebration of National Poetry Month. I have been writing poetry for as long as I can remember and it has always been a dream of mine for my passion to be recognized. Poetry has opened many doors for my future, and my dreams are finally coming true, as I hope yours do as well. I would like to thank my family for encouraging me to never give up, and I would like to send that message out to everyone! Follow your dreams, and no matter how many road blocks there are, you will always have the power to overcome them and achieve your dreams!

Untitled

She sits by the window, her eyes pale with tears
And watches the festival come to life.
She is seventy-three years, eight months and twenty two hours old.
She has a floral skirt on which barely brushes the crooked tips of her toes, and as she hears child laughter she pulls her ragged, fringed shawl closer over her lonely shoulders. She sighs.
A breath of summer wanders aimlessly into her house,
Bringing with it the smells of her childhood.
She remembers how when she was seven years old,
And three quarters, precisely,
She had been taken to the festival, and she
Remembers how, as a little girl, everything seemed so
Bright, enticing, so
Bracing, new, so
Captivating, earth-shattering, so
Safe. So familiar.
So lovely. So warm.
And at the end, she remembers how the fireworks—
Those indescribable beasts of passion that
Roar through the empty skies
And make their voices heard to all the stars—
She remembers how she wished,
If anything at all, she wished
Oh so badly she wished,
She could be like that.

Lily Rappaport

Road to Redemption

I'm on a road to redemption, seeking forgiveness for the wrongs I've done
My actions have been more predictable than the rising sun
But no longer shall I cause these misfortunes, a new era has begun
I have come to the understanding that I am the decisive element
That the things of the past are irrelevant
It is I in reality who decides the world, even the weather
Whether my life be joyous or miserable
Only I have the power to make my life into something incredible
I have the control to be a tool of pain or inspiration
To lead myself and others to despair or the fulfillment of their aspirations
I have the power to hurt or heal
I can shroud myself in calamity and dismay or reveal
The truth behind the lies
I have learned that we must love or die
We must treat others the way they should be treated in hopes that they will better themselves and reach their full potential
We must better this world, we cannot be defeated
Knowing is not enough, we must apply what we have learned
Willing is futile, we must do and look past our concerns
We do not need to go to a mad house to find disoriented minds
Our society is the mental institution of the universe
I've searched all my young life for signs and the purpose of life
Why we struggle why we go through strife
And have come to the conclusion that we're the masters of our own lives
How we are brought up, our culture, it means nothing
At the end of the day we control our actions and reactions
We control the path to the pursuit of happiness and our own satisfaction
In all, I have learned to let things go and to start anew
It took me awhile
But learn from my mistakes and my success and face adversity with a smile

Javier Altamiranda

Poetry is the centerpiece of my entire life. It is the outlet that allows me to express my happiness, my sorrow, my anger, even my sadness. Without it, I don't know how I would be able to live. My Mom and life experiences have molded me into the poet I am today. My goal is to be a world renowned poet, and to make not only myself but my family, especially my mother, proud.

Untitled

We can all say we have had amazing teachers
Or that we have had teachers we hate
There are always those one or two teachers who
are your favorite
The subject they teach may influence your choices
Or it might just be the kind of person they are
I love to sing and write
I have always had amazing teachers to push me to
keep writing
However, I have not always had an amazing vocal teacher
My vocal teacher pushes until I give what she wants
She never gives up on her vocal students
She has a way of making every day an adventure
you never know what silly things will happen during class
From the laughter to the serious moments
To the craziest moments and days ever
My vocal teacher keeps all her students focused and in line
There never could be another teacher who could replace her
I am thankful to have her as a teacher
She keeps me believing I can do anything I set my mind to
For that I am grateful to say she is my favorite teacher
And nobody can take that away from me

Krystal Hanson

Phoenix

Creative fire burns mightily
Sparked by the tip of a pen.
Consuming discrimination
And turning hate to dust.
A cleansing maelstrom of
Searing innovation sweeps
Through every heart here,
Burned to the ground, we
Are left with bare bones—
A clean, if ashen, slate for
Us to restart, to be reborn.
A chance to live up to our
Ideals, to right the wrongs
We've undergone and to
Learn from our mistakes.
Take heart everyone, we've
Been granted a second try.
A chance to get it right.

Katy Doty

I'm an eighteen-year-old with a passion for words. Writing saved my life and continually helps me attempt to unravel the mysterious workings of the world we live in. I write to find strength, despite adversity, empowerment in the face of fear, and most importantly, I write as a voice for those who haven't yet found the words they need. Next year I'll be studying computer science at Pacific University in Oregon (Go Boxers!) and, of course, writing in any free time I might have.

When a Teardrop Falls Somewhere, Something Inside Me Breaks

When a teardrop falls I feel myself drown,
in an ocean of sorrow.
I am living today so unprepared for tomorrow,
but the pain from yesterday is not in the
past. It is a fresh wound an open slash.
Every time I think of what could be and
what might not.
There's a burning in this cut a painful sting....
As if to remind me of what is there and
what is happening.
Do I scream? Do I run?
Would it be okay to cry? Why do I want to
die in your place?
I think of these thoughts and if they are
even a solution, to scream....
Would hurt my brain and make me sleep, to
just be reminded again of my pain in a dream.
Should I continue to cry I feel my eyes
are running dry, and with the tears come
a fear of losing you.
If I die I will leave behind so many
who love me who adore me and even someone
who will give it all for me.
If I die my spirit won't rest from being
depressed for leaving like I did.
My baby girl will not purposefully forget
about me, and grandma will be her only mommy.
Mommy will soak and cry at the loss of
her child, her strength turned to weakness.
Everyone will see the years fall on her ahead
of time... the constant questions from the
kids and long lost friends of where am I.

And boy will cry and his pain will hunt me
so I will not rest.

Cristina White

I hope everyone enjoyed my poem. Poetry is definitely one of my main stress relievers. This poem in specific was written during this very depressing moment in my life, a moment where a parent feels the loss of a child, a sister, a brother, a grandmom and a grandchild, an aunt and uncle, a nephew. Even though at this moment my son's heart beats within me his life is not promised. He is a victim of trisonny 18. This is for you baby boy. Mommy loves you, Sieul Anthony Ortiz.

The Scarlet River

It started off with rays of sun,
Changing to tears of rain.
We have nowhere to run,
but are trapped in a corner and going insane.
Blood trickling through the blocks of a silk black rose,
With stone cold eyes deeply staring,
Our shattered bones simply froze.
The depth of the pain
With a few scars to blame.
We float among the scarlet river
Of our own disintegrating flesh.
Surrounded by puddles says you're only a giver
As you do nothing with the fumes that enmesh.
Left with only our thoughts,
And nothing but to shake and shiver.
As we fade into the darkness,
Remember that we met through the rays of sun.

Kassidy Jones

First and Last Moment

I smiled the first time I looked in your eyes
Shedded a little tear, as time passed by
Enjoyed the first moment that we shared
From holding hands as the stars appeared
You held me tight and wouldn't let go
My heart sunk down deep into my soul
My body started shaking, and I wondered why
Then I heard you say: "It's that time to say goodbye"
My very first moment, and my last one too
How I meet this stranger right out of the blue
We made that connection and it went away
My first and last moment till this day

Hot Sexy Carmel

Fortune's Misfortune

Words are indescribable
To explain the pain we feel
When your casket was above us
We bowed our heads and kneeled
Tears came to our eyes
And to our surprise
This wasn't just a dream
Everything was really as it seemed

We've suffered and cried
While wondering why
You had to be taken from us
We'll never forget you
And it'll be tough to get through
But you'll remain in our hearts forever

In those eighty-three days
A hospital bed was where you laid
Unable to speak
Because your body was weak
Our ears became deaf
We couldn't believe you left
But we're glad you're finally at rest

We play reruns in our heads
Of everything you said
And we'll always remember
Your sense of humor
Your kind words and actions
And the memories that we'll cherish forever

Jodesha Yu Tan

The Museum

Behold the mural before you,
See the majesty?
A joy to behold and a wonder to see.
Smiling faces and beautiful places.
A companion around every corner, merely a casual conversation away.
Whisk me away to that wonderful state, to bliss, to fortune, fortune of the soul!
Take me down the rabbit hole,
And I'll never want again,
But please, lean closer, dare you hear
The snickers, the sneers of those who seem dear?
Have you, would you try and delve deeper, to see, to know?
Do you really want to?
Sure, it seems nice, a vision to be blessed,
A portrait of perfection, but dare you scratch the paint?
You may try to see, to carry on despite, to try to do the thing that's right,
Let's paint over and start anew! Bring the vision back to view!
But time is still, history is set, the canvas you see is no longer wet,
But take your chance, if you please
I'll hope the best, you will succeed.

Sierra Deterding

Man

One man over another,
society's ruled,
only the strong can survive.

The cost of a life,
one eternity for another,
just when do we cross the line?

Lies, betrayal,
society's raged by sickness,
with each lifetime we are faced.

No man can forfeit,
a fight of his own,
head and heart he is faced.

Judgment fills our heads,
explications we are supposed to fit,
society's lost its fight.

Hatred and despair,
dark emotions we are faced,
how did man lose his way?

Temptations all around,
man cannot resist,
society, the devil holds slave to his hand.

Power and lust,
this race man is faced,
he must finish first.

No man can claim to be equal,
if we all strive,
to be better than the next.

For this lifetime man is faced,
please sign here on the dotted line,
let's shake hands with the devil.

Marguerite Hiltermann

Entangled Metal

Watch as they dance, entangled metal
Dust, it will always try to settle
Swirl around, feet from the earth
They despise each other's birth
Two men, they respect each other
Yet never refer to brother
Both have experienced this
Life and death, they know the risks
One sports a star, the other a cross
Neither of them have a coin to toss
One fights for his mother, the other for his father
With all the hate, neither of them can accept a proffer
Who live in close, yet so distant lands
Appears that "great" men have gifted hands
They say it's for the kids and wives
But really it becomes their lives
Ashes to ashes, dust to dust
They hold on, aren't in any rush
They see each other come and go
Oh, why must time be so slow?
Finally, now, they touch
Just a tap, not too much
But that which spins, heart of the beast
Collide in a fiery feast
They kiss the earth, smoke and blaze
No one can make out the haze
Metal to metal, gun to gun
It comes along, that neither have won

Kirby Kinghorn

Memories of Mom

I remember when you chased
All the monsters from my room,
And made up funny stories for me
When I had the flu.

I remember when you told me
How the earth is round,
And that gravity's the reason
That we stay on the ground.

I remember how you cried with me
Whenever I was sad,
And then you made me laugh again
'Till I was feeling glad.

I remember how you read
The Bible to me every night,
And told me how that Jesus Christ
Should be my first delight.

I remember how I knelt and prayed
That when I had kids I'd be,
The best mom in the world to them
Just like you are to me.

Elisabeth Grace

I wrote this poem as a Mother's Day present for my mom. I will be forever grateful that she chose life when she had me. Mom, for all the things that you have done for me, for all of the sacrifices that you have made, and for all the things that you have taught me, I thank you with all of my heart. I would not be who I am today without your influence. I love you!

Heart & Head

Head says one thing
Heart does another
Logic loses power
And spirit takes me over

My heart knows no limits
For its power is endless
But to follow through means ignoring any instinct

Though crazy at times
My head follows order
This thought goes here, that thought goes there
No room for nonsense
(At least in theory)

Now put them together
And surely you can't go wrong
Yet they are like enemies
My heart and my head
Never in agreement
Forever in battle

Izzy Allen

Dark Magic

My soul is damaged,
My heart is shattered,
You've ruined my life.
You think you're high-powered,
But you're a thief.
I gave you my heart at the dawn of time,
However it was a mistake.
You lied indefinitely.
The spear of a broken heart
With the writings of dark magic.
That magic is the lies of your love.
The icy, cold wind whips my soul.
Your dark magic made me fall in the beginning,
But now I see right through you.
I've finally defeated your magic
with all my strength and strength of many.
I'm lifted up from my black hole
Of a lifeless body.
Reborn to the truth for a better life.

Alexander Hansen

My Darkness

Hello, my darkness, I see you've returned.
You've come back to mark me,
Come back to burn.

You're taking my past,
Throwing it in my face,
You catch me at my weakest,
Full embrace.

You drive me crazy,
Although I act sane.
I just want to rid of you,
I can't take the pain.

You see my darkness,
My sorrow, my hate.
When I'm left to think,
You're something I create.

You're only there when I begin to reflect,
No happiness amidst me.
You're that empty space in my mind,
Those memories I see.

I diminish you, darkness,
I kill you with love.
For the tears you bring me
Are something I've had enough of.

Tori Kalbach

Embrace Uncertainty

Every day starts with this blur
Never seems to get clearer
Or brighter
Only blurrier

That constant hum and purr
Of my motors pumping
Pulsing, throbbing
Working,
On the unanswered questions
Of Uncertainty.

But there are always competitions—
Brain and heart
Politics and art

Serious controversies
Phobias of ideas as ancient as Cleopatra
Returning
Back to self-harm and anorexia
All are chancy
Which makes you antsy.

You begin appearing as Miss Mona Lisa,
Hiding behind a simple smile, just like her.
When deep down you feel like the sir
In the scream,
Who's losing an airstream.

Now's the time to dream
And scheme;
Along with uncertainty.

Monica Mazur

I wrote "Embrace Uncertainty" with the message about not stressing out about what's to come in your future, whether it's tomorrow, a year from now, or ten. I've always found myself to have a definite plan before acting on something; however, I've come to realize that you can have goals, like for me it's attending my dream college in a few years, but sometimes you need to work with what you have and simply enjoy yourself and the people around you.

Different Sides to the Same Feeling

Are we so different?
We all wear the same frown;
We all walk down our streets
Practically screaming about
How much we hate this town.

What's left here
But lost teens
And broken window screens?
There's nothing left here but us
And our need to leave.

When we're gone,
We'll all forget each other
And the labels we gave.
We'll move on to better days;
We all have a world to save.

Kira Trivette

Pre-Calc

Exactly the same:
Walk in,
Sit down,
Take notes,
Start assignment?

Day- after- day -
Monday: Tuesday: Wednesday: Thursday: Friday?
(-5,4); m=-2/5
To....,
Day or morrow -
3x + 3y +24x-18y+24 = 0

Solve -
Day-after-day
Thursday: Friday? Saturday? Sunday?
SOLVE -

Carolina Valadez

A special thanks goes out to my high school teachers for letting me write poems about them and their class. And by saying that, this is how this poem came about. I wrote this poem while sitting in my high school pre-calc class. The poem first was written as a joke to my math teacher, but every time I worked on the poem, it started to look good. This poem doesn't have any significant message but if one rereads the poem, they may see a message; that math is around us all the time.

This World

In this world, the beautiful places I've been and seen.

In this world we wonder if there's life in another world,
probably wondering if we are here.

In this world life is too short, you got to make it last before it's
too late.

In this world we also wonder what the meaning of life is.
Maybe the meaning was in front of us this whole time and we
just didn't see it.

In this world there are good times and bad times. We must
remember only the good times.

We live and learn with our mistakes. There are many mysteries
in this world and life. Let our minds feel free to explore and
discover something new.

In this world I want to make a difference.

In this world I want to make my life worth living.

Arthur Krimberg

Nature Listen to the wind

Touch the ground beneath your feet,
Feel the strength within.
Look at the winding river,
See its ever-changing course.
Watch the fire burning,
Understand it's light and life.
Know each of these are alive.
Stop looking with just your eyes.
Feel with your soul,
The power and energy they have.

Ashlee Spears

My poems mean the world to me. They are my way of releasing my thoughts. In the real world I'm shy and not very confident in myself, but in my poems I'm not shy. Thanks to my mom and dad I continue to write. My best friend helped me gain the courage to do this. Her continued support made me proud of my poems. Thank you for this amazing opportunity.

A Tale

Blooming tail, curling claw
And glowing eyes downcast
The kind ruler forced to roam
Because of the dark past

Far from home, sad and lone
Running hither, yon and far
The fighter, the shade
And stars will play their past

Seeking peace, seeking rest
Dark will earn the citadel
Bringing hope, making lovers
Knowing none will bale

Blazing wixen, snarling dag
And green-eyed student follow
Clawing, biting, flying, fighting
Doomed to never know

Hating hate, loving naught
Painful blue tears fall
Defending all, life distraught
Heeding wisdom's call

Forgot must be the price
For peace belongs to some
Because sought was the prize
Yours is rest, oh gentle one.

Rayanne Robison

I discovered my fondness and aptitude for poetry purely by accident. Once I got started though, I was hooked. "A Tale" is based on a story I am trying to write. In the poem, I tried to express not only a synapsis, but also the trials of being the good guy, something I think a lot of stories really miss and/or misunderstand.

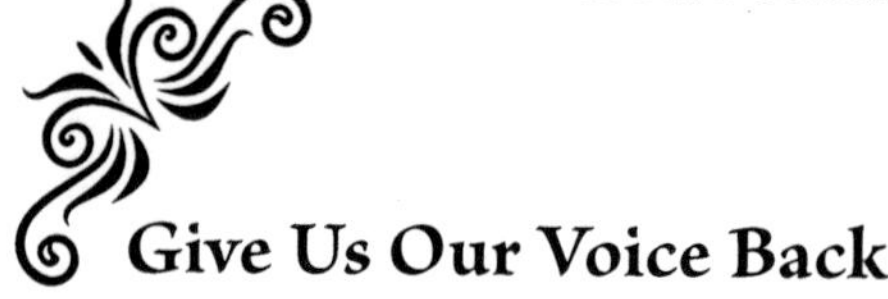

Give Us Our Voice Back

Give us our voice back, please hear our cry
For those of us still fighting, and honor to those who die
We need some justice, we need a hand
Let the court hold us up and together we can stand

With both shame and fear, we run into the night
battered and bruised, with children filled with fright
We go into hiding for crimes that are not ours
but those of an abuser who seems to hold all the power

We file the paperwork, hoping it will keep us safe from the pain
But it is only paper and truly not meant to restrain
We bury our friends, those of us who ran
The system failed them and cycle starts again

You wonder why we are silent, why some of us do not tell
It is fear of retaliation, of the abuser that keeps us in this hell
So many are gone, they thought they could be free
That the courts would protect them, but that was not reality

If you do not convict them, and lock them far away
The abuser will go after the focus of his prey
He will make them suffer and kill them if he chooses
Don't seem so surprised, but the victim, always loses

Stop the cycle and enforce a tougher policy
Domestic violent is a vicious killer, in this, our country
Don't let one of you look away, not one more time
But severely punish, those who commit this horrid crime

Help protect the victims and lock away the one who breaks the law
And hear the cried of victims, let us answer every single call

No longer allowing an abuser to walk free and on the street
To harm another victim, for it is the abuser we must defeat

Deonna Hampton

I write from the heart. My father always told me to follow my heart and always listen to your heart. It is all about emotions, experiences. I am blessed to have the support and love of a wonderful husband and my children. I married a man, and just like my father . . . I followed my heart. My strength and courage to write this poem came from deep within for the women and children who are often not heard. I hope I can give them a voice through this poem.

I Love You

Sweetheart, do you know how lonely I am?
Can you hear me when I cry?
Or feel the pain of my aching heart?
Can you see how empty my arms are?
Oh, to hold you, but you're away so far
If I could tell you, and you could hear
I'd say, I love you, precious one so dear
You're all I ever wanted, always it was you
All things in life have a purpose it seems
Thank you, sweetheart, for the beautiful dreams
I replay the memories over and over again
It's just a fleeting picture of us, back then
If there's a tomorrow I'll miss you still
And remember your sweetness, I always will
Yet, even now, I look and I'll find
You walking, through the shadows of my mind
We are as the tumbleweed, blown by the wind
Carried to somewhere, where we've never been
Maybe to paradise or somewhere in between
There hasn't been a day, that I'm not sad
But I'm so thankful, for the time we had
I shall keep your memory in my heart
I shall hold it like a cherished thing apart
I'll take the time to search for you in my dreams
I'll walk with you in the meadows and by a stream
I would chase the winds to the ends of the earth
To be with you and all that you're worth.

Lisa Gasswint

To my precious husband, Luther Brumbalow
From your wife, Teddi

You're the Love of My Life

I love your eyes,
Looking into them each and every day I see into your soul.
The first day I saw you was love at first sight.
We shared life together;
You knew my secrets and I knew yours.
When you kissed me my smile got brighter,
When you held onto me I wanted you forever.
Our love was like a never-ending river,
My heart never stopped beating when you were around.
But when you left it stopped beating tell I saw next,
All my passion for you was like you and me could stop the world together.
We were one together,
And I will love you forever until the end of time.

Hannah Sathre

God's Gift to You

I lay
I wonder
Why is my mind blank?
I see myself around,
Or in the middle of
My comfort zone

It is the people,
I swear the audience
Smolders my passion
Into wit
As my body separates from my sole

Handicapped by measure
I retreated into solitude
Taking away the gift
Thy Lord has given
And smothers it almost to extinction

Then now as I am telling you
I break through the smog of depression
And burst through
Giving what we all want,
Gratification for oneself

When others' eyes open and read this truth
They too are stripped of their blanket
To hide behind
And find themselves open
For their treasure of life

For now, I found mine
And I will hold it
With a firm sweaty, grasp
As I see what the world
Was hiding from me?

I will tell you in written word
When you find what drives your passions
Face it, feel it, live it,
It is your gift from our Lord.

Amen

Sandra Jacobson

I believe everyone has a talent, some just don't know yet what theirs are. I have been writing for years and have been published several times with many awards, but when my Back Disease got worse my mind became clouded with pain. My talent, my passion of writing is also my healer and so I begin again, with a new outlook and more Poetry to heal the reader and the writer.

War

Bells are clanging,
bombs keep banging.
Kids are screaming,
while the dead are dreaming.
Stealth could save you,
as killers crave you.
You try to hide,
within deep tides.
You want it to end,
as your life starts to bend.
People are fighting,
a nation uniting.
All peace is lost,
at such a tough cost.
War causes distress,
in our world that's a mess.

Calina Edsell

Hi, I'm Calina and I'm fourteen years old. I wrote my poem because I wanted to write poetry about the world and life in general. I use poetry like people use religion. I don't have faith in religion though. I have many more poems but "War" is a bit different from my others. My hobbies include photography, poetry (of course), and singing. My family means everything to me, including friends. I wrote "War" with so much seriousness. Poetry and music mean so much to me. I'm amazed judges even considered it though. It makes me proud of my writings.

Dreamful Flight

When I dream I fly away to another time and day.
I see so many strange, odd things,
which set my trapped sad spirit free.

Bermuda grass, a sharp sad thing. May apple blooms make me want to
sing. A leaping frog, so green and round, makes me laugh and flip my
frown. No wonder dreams are such a trip. I hear the rain go
drip, drop, drip.

Nothing ever will go wrong when my dream is going on. Now I
understand the words "I can fly like the birds!"

I never will forget that flight on that cold April's night.

When time elapses into mist and nothing matters, only this. My dream
will be my state of mind. I will know what is inside. The hearts of all
will give me strength.

But now it's over, I will wake.

Danielle C. Brooks

I started writing poetry when I was eight. I was inspired by a poem that I read in an LDS magazine and by my older sister's writing. I think that poetry is a good way to express feelings or just random thoughts. I'm home-schooled but I go to a commonwealth that some friends started. I enjoy singing, dancing, acting and of course writing poetry. I also write songs and stories. Poetry is a great joy in my life. I wrote this particular poem in a journaling class. We incorporated the names of color samples. I enjoyed this assignment a lot.

Just to Say...

Your smile, oh that smile
shining so bright
and stretches out a mile wide,
makes me think you're a star in my sight.

Your deep dark eyes
stare through my sole,
they make you look wise
and warm not cold.

Your skin is so soft
not a flaw in sight,
it sparkles like a moth
and your black hair adds to your height.

And now I am watching you walk away
But I am wishing that you would stay so I can say...

Cylie Newman

Just Let Me Fly

Just let me fly, fly away from this all
These bright lights and these foolish calls
Let's get away, away from today
Make this in vain of yesterday
Let her speak, raise the champaign
Take it out of this glass she stained
If you may please she sounds far from humane
Let's shut the drum to our ears,
Forget the world was even here
And them speaking don't let them interfere
And to those sightseers those budgeteers
Let's runaway, away from the noise
Let's restrain from the talking in terms of the voice
And so on let the moment takes it course
If time only understood
Let's shut our eyes picture the clashing
Let's close our eyes and regain our conscience
That's dreaming right
Wait, that sounded better in my mind
Let's not walk, walk towards the end
Where lights are brighter and they tend to offend
Those
Who actually enjoy its intend
To rush the hour to comprehend.
Just let me fly, fly away
I'd spread the bones and make them wings
I'd jump in the sense of being blind
I'd shout till my lungs resign
And when my mind says stop
I'll remind myself
I'm resting
I'll stack that on the shelf as well.

Angelica Enith Diaz

Stronger Than Today

As you lay there,
Asleep in my bed
I sit in amazement,
I wonder what is ahead

I smile about yesterday,
And what today has brought me
And wish it for tomorrow,
The future I can't see

For it has love,
Gives happiness to my heart
I refuse old wounds and jealousies,
To rip this love apart

I am working hard
On making things right,
Healing those scars, you help me,
Without anger or spite

You are by my side,
I can see this now
Strong and fearless with love for me,
I give you this vow

That whatever crosses our paths,
Or tried to get in our way
My love for you in every tomorrow,
Will be ever so stronger than today

Randy M. Stevens

I have always dabbled in writing, but after going through the horrific events of 9/11 and losing friends that worked at WTC in NYC, I used writing as an outlet. Once I found love, the words just kept coming.

Inward Embers

People burn like embers.
Some of us burn in passion.
People burn like embers.
Some of us burn in passion.
Some of us burn in dreams.
Some of us burn as both of them together.
And to us life is like a liquid oil canvas tracing
our moments as we the swimming embers
are defining it as it defines us in life's stream.
While we're walking, while in a dream.
That's why the skies are threaded in the
dreams of divinity, as the stars are their
embroidery.

Derek Walsh

Truth Is ...

The truth is,
I have a hard time expressing what I'm truly feeling,
But there is one feeling that isn't so hard for me to show,
and that is my love for you.
'Cause I'm truly and madly in love with you,
and not just in love with you as a person,
but also I'm in love with the way you speak
and the way you think.
It drives me insane and I think about you 24/7,
but I also love it 'cause it's only you that I think about, no one else.
The truth is,
I love you in every way that a woman could love a man,
from personal to universal,
but most of all unconditional,
that I truly feel this way for another guy...

Austin Daniels

Love's Control

Soft as a whisper of wind through the trees,
Gentle as the falling of new snow,
Sneaking upon one so quiet and quick,
This love that is found will blossom and grow.

Feeling the touch as light as a feather,
The heart skips a beat at the very sound
Of the voice that quietly passionately calls me.
Love beckons to realize what has been found.

Chances are made to be taken with hopes
Of good things to happen without any doubts.
Though fear often causes much hesitation,
The desires within roll away all the clouds.

Given another chance to love unconditionally,
It can all go away with the wrong frame of mind.
But open the heart to a new day dawning,
Love rises again and can never be bound.

Jeanette Bailey

Whether a song or a poem, the spoken word has always touched me deeply. I wrote my first poem at eight years old and my first gospel song at ten years old. I have always felt things deeply, and expression through words is the easiest way to convey how I feel. I live in Houston, TX, where I work in accounting. My son Jobey is the light in my life. Life is good. I hope the words I've written touch you as deeply as the inspiration that caused me to write them has touched me. Be blessed!

Mirror Me

When I look in the mirror, do you know what I see?
A sad pathetic little girl looking back at me

To me, not much to look at, though
Pretty is what they say
To me she seems unhappy every single day

How can that be possible? Some people may reply
With a smile for us and a bubbly tone
Every time she passes by
How can that girl they talk about
How can she be me?
Yes, outside on my face may show
A smile for all to see
But on the inside all the time is hurt and misery

With practice has grown perfection
I've perfected my projection
Of what I want you to see, not the real unhappy me

I just can't seem to do it, I can't let people know
That the real me spirits broke quite a while ago
So with a smiling face and cheerful word
Happiness I may show
But remember everything you see isn't always so

So continue I do, put on the face
That people have grown to know
A happy, bubbly, together girl is what I try to show
Soon I am quite certain, this pain will go away
Of forever searching for peace of mind
Every single day

The courage I need, I soon will find
I leave all of this pain behind
Then finally I will be free, at last
I won't be so unhappy

The coward's way out, it just might be
But I hate who I am, so don't judge me

Debbie Sellas

My name is Debbie. I'm forty-five and have been expressing my feelings through poetry since I was quite young. My poetry allows me to verbalize my feelings no matter what they may be. My family is my greatest support—Mom and Dad, Andrea and Raymond Jr.; my stepdad Andres, who unfortunately is no longer with us; my sister Susie and family; my brother Ray and family; and my wonderful son Phillip Andrew and daughter-in-law Natalie who have blessed me with my greatest treasure, my grandson Lukas Alexander. Even with all my blessings, my depressive state brings me to darkness. Thank God for poetry as an outlet.

My Survivor

You are no longer the boy I remember
You are grown
A man now
Responsible and reliable
I know
That you will never let anyone down
You have had hardships
You have survived them all
That is what you are
A survivor
You always were
And you always will be
No matter where the tide takes you
You will come home unscathed
Shattered is a word to describe a broken mirror
But not one to describe your sprit
You are strong
You are you
Never let anything change you
My survivor

Emily Brown

Butchie

You're on my mind
And you're in my dreams
Most of all you're in my heart
I wish we didn't have to be apart
If I could just touch
Your soft silky fur one more time
My heart would be content
But instead my heart has a missing piece
That could only be fixed if you were here
My dear little cocker spaniel
I wish you were here

Delaney Borenstein

This poem is in loving memory of my dog Butchie. He was a great dog. He died in 2004 at age seventeen—the day the Red Sox won the World Series. I am so proud I can get this poem published especially since it means so much to me. I started writing poetry two years ago because people were teasing me about my stutter and writing poetry was the only way I had to express myself. I have enjoyed writing poetry ever since and hopefully always will.

Our Song

The song reminds me of you
And all the things we used to do
Where did we go wrong
The song reminds me of the time
When I was yours and you were mine
But now it's gone

The song that I learned from you
I was the one you gave it to
So what went wrong
The song we played most every night
It brought us to a whole new height
But it's all gone

I felt your warmth when I would hear
The chorus sweeping through my ear
This is all wrong
But now I tremble when it starts
And I feel myself fall apart
Because you're gone
When I listen to our song

Alena Lotter

Just Him

He makes me feel so alive
He makes me feel safe in his arms
When we are by the trees that thrive
When I look into his eyes all I see are charms

His kiss takes me to another world
His touch makes my heart flutter
I just want to crawl into his arms and stay curled
I see his eyes and I shudder

I love him dearly, I truly do
So when he asks I say no duh
And if he doesn't believe me, boo hoo
I just kiss him and listen to his "huh?"

His smile is the best
His voice is a flowing river
His eyes are the forest
His love is an ever-going shiver

To think I have found him
After so many years of chasing my dove
So whenever I see him
I cherish the moment so I will never lose my love.

McKenzie Miller

Untitled

If I were a flower,
I'd want you to be the spring shower.
If I were the moon,
I'd want you to surround me with stars that don't gloom.
If I were the darkness,
I'd want you to be there to hold,
But now things are getting oh so cold.

If I were blind,
I'd want you to be my eyes.
If the world was going to end,
I'd want to be next to you and live.
If I were this poem,
I'd want you to read me over and over again.

What-ifs are filling my mind,
Thinking what would really happen if I died.
I know for sure that you would cry,
So for now what if I were the ocean?
Would you go for a swim?
Don't worry love,
I'll keep you afloat.
You never have to worry about going deep under again.

If I were a butterfly,
I'd want you to be my flower.
And if I were a flower,
I'd want you to be my spring shower.

Victoria Holderbaugh

My Butterfly

As a child, I had a dream
that would not go away
It only grew, ingrained in my
Brian, perhaps in the womb.

Playing on a cliff, a grassy flat
Next to the sea.
So much fun I was having,
Me and my orange ball.

My ball bounced over the cliff
Down to the sea.
I followed,
Falling, falling, falling.

All I wanted was my orange ball.
Fear, fear, fear.
I was heading for the rocks below.
Then with a sigh and a
Breath, the hands of God
Moved and into an orange
butterfly I grew.

Now I flutter my wings up
Back to the grassy flat I once
Knew as a child!

John W. Za'ber

When Anger Takes Over

Stress might just be an understatement
You know you wanna get rid of your anger
Feel in power
Feel strong
Prey on smaller
Push them around
As if a rag doll
Don't think just go on your emotions of anger
Make that anger go to power
You feel better after one hit yet you don't stop
Feeling in power takes over
Hit after hit after hit
I could see the satisfied look on your face
Swinging me
Smacking me
Plain and simple
Hope your happy
Hope the adrenaline was worth it
That night now haunts my dreams

Hailey Feind

Potential

Hot coals in a fire pit used long ago
Crave wood and tinder to restart
Just a bit will cause an explosion
Of heat and beauty
A bit more will cause the fire to expand

But for now, the coals wait
Wait for the twigs nearby to fall
Wait for the new warmth to start
Just waiting
Never cooling
Never going out
Always there

Jennifer Carter

All of my life, I've seen people take different things from one experience. From one poem, there are many meanings. I wrote this with one thought in mind, yet everyone who reads it thought of something different. This poem helped me express something only I knew, as many of mine do. For me, this is one of the best ways to express myself, ever since I was little. Poetry means an untamed freedom to me. I'll never give it up.

Change

Every generation sees the last as old, outdated, behind the times.
Each blames the last for all the current problems.
As a result, each strives to make a difference....
Things change, but the problems remain.

A number of individuals stand out in each generation.
Bridging the gap, between past and present.
Still, there is stress, tension, uprising....

Yet, in spite of all the stress of change....
There are individuals who have performed great jobs.
Showing dedication to reach the goal.
We see them every day without,
most of the time, even knowing who they are.

When we finally realize the significance of their work,
they've already moved on... new places, new jobs, new lives.
They've done so much, but still there seems so much left to do.
We wonder if we'll ever see them again

If they do return, will they be the same?

John Colyer II

Growing up, we moved quite a bit over the years. Friends came with each move. More friends went away. Raised with strong, faithful believers and books of all kinds feeding my imagination, I set ideals for living a great, blessed life. I just had to write about how awesome and beautiful this world really is. Continually urged to pursue it, I simply wrote to entertain those around me. Thinking it was worth professional consideration...just seems like so much flattery. Imagine my awe in finding that others out there actually enjoy my work and want to see more.

A Love Song to J. Alfred Prufrock

I remember when I met you.
Walking through bodies, I brushed aside your leather elbows
and asked why the floorboards looked like maps
of places that you would rather be.
You said, "I'm sorry. I never liked Michelangelo."

So I took the pins out of my voicebox
and broke the hands off the clocks
so we would have time for everything.

You walked me home that night
and memorized the color of my front door
and one day, you lost yourself in the streets and alleys
kept your hands so deep in your pockets
that they couldn't point you in the direction
of the inaudible question I hoped you would ask
because I wanted to give it a thunderclap answer.

Instead, you walked to the beach with your trousers rolled
looked at the waves and felt your fingers turn to claws.
I still go to the beach every day
in hopes that I see your bent backbone
listening for the music that deafened you.

When I walk over subways, I mistake the trains
for your heart, buried below silence and cement
I look at the floors too, now.
They look like the spines of the books you lent me
that I have not dared to return yet.

If you look at me one last time,
I want to whisper that I, too,
feel like a crab being crushed
between the fingers of a mermaid
but I'm afraid that if I dare to,
no words will leave my mouth.
Just tendrils of yellow smoke.

Claire McDonald

The Last Dance

Every breath I take
gets knocked out of me.
Every step I make,
I fall to my knees.

I cannot speak or think,
for my body moves to the rhythm.
I cannot stop dancing to even breathe.
I give up and let my body not miss a beat.

The words of a song flows past me,
I longed for them, not wanting them to leave.
This is not who I am, not how I want it to be.
Everything I know and believe

starts to fade away
with every step that I make.
A path that was for me to find my way,
I am lost with each breath I take.

This is the last of me.
The final steps of the rhyme.
This is who I am made to be.
The final dance of my time.

Allisha Szcodronski

A Mother's Love

I'll always love my mama, she's my favorite girl
I'll always love my mama she brought me in this world.
Those were the words to a familiar song that people used to sing some time ago, but I will forever love my mother and I want the world to know. I was raised by my grandmother from the time I was a baby.
And because of her prayer and teachings she taught me how to be a lady. I oftentimes heard Grandma while down on her bended knee
I couldn't quite understand—why is she talking to God about me?
Well I never would have stopped my grandma or tried telling her what to do, because little did I know it was her prayer that would get me through.
I've noticed a lot of parents and children never seem to see eye to eye well, that's the devil's plan; he don't care if we live or die.
But the Bible says to train up a child in the way he should go and when he gets old he will not depart well, some parents train and train and that child still grows up and breaks that mother's heart.
But as long as Mama knows that Jesus will be a rock in a weary land mama can sit back and relax and place that child in the palm of God's hand.
So there's no need in wondering why some parents or children act the way the do, don't you read the Bible because every word in there is true.
It clearly talks about how mothers will turn against their daughters and fathers against their sons but if you put your trust in Jesus then your battles are already won.
Now, nobody said that raising children would be an easy task,
but God said whatever we need all we have to do is ask.
Therefore, I will always love my mother and I wouldn't have it any other way and if I didn't learn but ONE thing I at least learned how to pray.
See Mama taught me things she knew would carry me through and had I not listened to mama I wouldn't have known what to do.
Now we didn't always see eye to eye or even get along
because sometimes Mama was right and sometimes mama was wrong.
But I did just what the words in the Bible say—
I looked past mama's faults and continued to love her each and every day.

I never disrespected her nor told her what I am or not going to do
That would have been a no, no and out the window I would have flew.
Well now that I'm grown with a family of my own I'm going to do the same things my grandma did and truth be told I will not be bossed around by mine or somebody's else's kid.
Now there will be those days when you don't want to listen to mama or even take her motherly advice and sometimes when that happens you'll end up paying an ugly price.
They're talking about all the problems happening over in the middle east, but because I listened to Mama I know how to pray for peace.
They're talking about the high percentage rate of single mothers raising their children all alone, but I listened to Mama when she said, "Baby God sits high up on His throne."
They talk about food prices, budget cuts, and job loss, but I listened when Mama said "Baby remember that for you and I Jesus died upon the cross." She said, "Whenever you're faced with difficulty, always remember that God has the whole world right in the palm of his hand so all you have to do is put your trust in him and not man."
Well I can't dot my I's or cross my T's like Mama used to do
BUT I can believe that prayer will see me through.
So if your mom is still alive and she's kicking and doing well
keep on trusting in God because He will never fail.
If your mom has left and you feel she's left you behind
put your arms around yourself and say Jesus I'm glad you're mine.
And if you are a man or woman with no children but you came to earth by way of a mother, whether she's good, bad, right or wrong, God said to love her.

Renita V. Walker

My mother had me at a very young age so my grandmother raised me. A lot of ways my grandma had I didn't understand because she migrated from the South with very little education. My grandma was a very religious person. We can choose our clothes, the foods we eat but we can't pick or choose our parents. My mom and I grew up together; she was an only child so sometimes we'd say we were sisters instead of mother and daughter. It was grandmother who started me writing inspirational poetry. So to my grandma, rest in peace, Noma—I'll love you always.

Zoo Animal

I am a lonely caged animal,
An attraction in the zoo.
The people walk by,
Rattle my cage,
Just to make me mad!

I am a lonely caged animal,
And this anger festers inside me.
My tortured soul watches
As the people walk by,
Rattling my cage.

I am a lonely caged animal,
But no one does see.
This anger that does overwhelm me,
Some day...
I'll finally set free!

Samantha D. Tamuschy

I Miss You

My dear sweetheart,
I miss you. I want to be with you and hold you. I want to gently touch your face and cup your cheek in my hands as I look into your beautiful eyes. I want to snuggle and cuddle with you, to just be close to you. I want to rub your legs and stare across the table at a restaurant. I want others in the restaurant to be jealous of our intimacy and our tender affection for one another. I want to lie next to you in front of a fire and gaze into your eyes while I rub your back. I want you to know how much I cherish and adore you. I want to give my heart to you. I want your heart, I want it all.

With fond affection and loving thoughts.

Latifah Williams

Don't Go

Hold me tightly,
Kiss me gently.
Grab my hand,
Grasp my heart.
You stop the tears,
Start the laughter.
Make me smile
Keep me from hurting.
Always knowing
What to say.
Never keeping
Any feelings in.
You know my feelings
You hear my thoughts
Keep me close.
Please don't let go.

Erica Mercure

I first began writing stories and poetry when I was about eight years old. I realized it was a passion of mine early in my freshman year of high school. My good friend Tara has helped me immensely. She is a great inspiration and has encouraged me along the way.

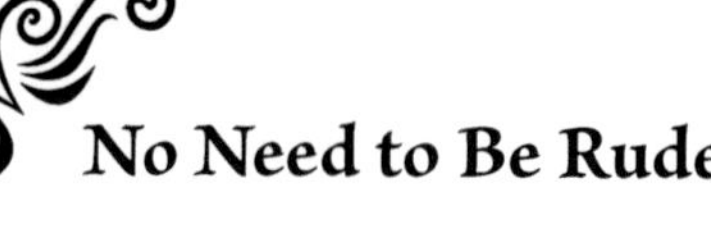

No Need to Be Rude

saw me the other day, said it was only yesterday
I wondered if I'd ever hear from your again
you said you've met someone new
said that love was possible, that he got thru
then asked me what I've been up to

couldn't make out your eyes from the sun
it overtook all I saw, overtook all of my sight
you're no longer my one true friend
though my memories of you are still bright

I turned away to never remember you
and the time just flew, I had forgotten you
like a photograph so rare my heart seemed renewed
I hid away from danger, like your passion and your anger
I've been weary of flawless strangers

everywhere I turn, there's a back against the wall
it's always been an eye for an eye, constant and unforgiving
there's little else to do but listen
and I was under the impression you were the only one
who got the twisted humours of my loving

believed it was time that we could speak like adults
that we could speak freely with no need to be rude
no need to turn our dialogue crude
you're trying to make something out of what's not there
trying to piece together your excuses out of thin air

maybe I jumped the gun, maybe my reasons are obtuse
or maybe I am to blame
I'm only ever trying to make it out okay
there's nothing much to lose
when nothing has gone your way

George Wood

Dreams Make Us Up

In light or dark, I can't ever
picture us apart. In big places
with people all around, you're the one
whose face stands out in the
crowd, like everything else around is
invisible and it seems as if we're
the only ones around. In small places
we meet again, smiles on our face,
with tears of disgrace. Where has time
gone, it's got away, we weren't able to
catch it and now we ended up this
way. When I told you, I only wanted
you, what didn't you get, it wasn't a
lie, it wasn't a threat it was our
relationship I didn't want to forget.
I dream of you, our memories that were
made and I have watched them all
fade like old pictures in the rain. I dream,
I dream, I dream hoping we will be together
again, 'cause after all you're the one who
had my heart, whom I loved most of
all. People tell me it's okay and it's
just a relationship that wasn't meant
for me, so I put a smile on to hide my emotions,
and act as if everything's going my way, but on
the inside I'm dying to say, I still love
him in every way, no matter if he hurt
me in anyway, my feelings for him will
always feel the same. So I dream
every night of us together. Maybe hoping
things will get better.

Morgan Mendyk

I'm a freshman in high school. I am age fourteen, and my birthday is June 23rd. I have been writing my entire life basically, but just within the past year I got more in depth with it. Poetry helps me express my feelings/emotions and get them out on paper. I will continue to do writing as a passion as my life goes on. It's just something I will forever enjoy.

Nostalgia

Open the cedar chest
Memories inside
The book my grandma read to me
The rock I found by the seaside
Pictures of my childhood house,
That tire swing beneath the tree
The bonnets and pinafores I used to wear
A drawing done by me
Elementary and high school awards and pins
Letters and poems written by friends
I just want to lock my whole being
In the cedar chest
And never want my memories to end....

Rebekah Sharon Palmer

It was late one night and I was struggling over research that had to do with a school project. The content I had chosen to write about gave a grim outlook on American society so I started thinking about good memories from my childhood. I closed my eyes and wished there was a door in every house one could open into another world made up of that person's good experiences, and they could stay as long as they needed. I opened my eyes and penned this poem.

If You Think Before You Speak

Sticks and stones may break my bones,
We've heard that rhyme before,
But words can really hurt you,
They can cut you to your core.

Childish taunts and bullying,
Can damage a young mind.
They will gnaw at a person's soul,
'Til no hope is left behind.

From the tears and sadness,
Hatred will start to grow,
Without warning it may come,
To strike its vengeful blow.

Everyone will wonder why,
And never stop to think.
It was caused by the thoughtless words,
That pushed them to the brink.

If you think before you speak,
And answer yourself true.
How would it make you feel
If your mean words were being said to you?

Mary Lindsay

I was born in Maryland in 1951, but was raised in Pocatello, ID. I came from a family of ten children, of which I am number four. Both of my parents have long since passed, but all of my siblings are still around. I am married to a retired sailor, have two daughters, four grandsons, one granddaughter, and two great-grandsons. This poem was inspired by the many needless school shootings that have taken place in the past several years, most of which were the result of verbal bullying.

Acts of Love

As I reminisce over the life I have lived, I must say that love has blessed me in many ways. It is unexplainable. It is a beautiful thing. It is...

Unchanging
By the world around you
And is limitless in its power
Covering
All multitudes of sin
And making our lives more abundant
Accepting
All races and genders
Regardless of age and our backgrounds
Redeeming
All the hope that was lost
Instilling grace into our lives
Assuring
We are safe and secure
Resting in its tenderness of peace
Suppressing
All negative aspects
Giving motivation to us all
Allowing
Us to be who we are
And not change for anything on earth
Surpassing
Any earthly treasure
Infinite to any currency
And lasting
A lifetime with whom
God chose to be the right one for you...

Rowdy D. Solomon Jr.

Poetry is not just words that I twist and craft to arouse or excite the reader, but it is rather a piece of my life shared with you through words. Every syllable is a beat of my heart. Every letter is a molecule that makes up my characteristics. All in all, poetry is my life, and my life is in my poetry.

Someday

Shadows stretched across the black and white
as Sunday's typeface leered, taunting me.
Twenty pages, I grimaced and sighed.
Flipped the pages. Do it now, today!

Varieties of black font exposed
themselves like legible bird droppings.
Overwhelmed, orbs rolled in their sockets.
The tissue for eminent despair.

Clutching an oversized java mug
I X'd numerous classified ads
as fluorescent yellow stung the air.
A dark revelation. I should pray.

I punched the ten and sipped the dark brew.
A voice! Brown liquid spattered the page.
I blurted, what? Then, what's the pay scale?
Someone said the, "Don't call us cliché."

To my chagrin, that was all I heard
and then silence. I groaned in dismay.
Overwhelmed with bills. Chair tilted back.
What to do, would they ever get paid?

Oh yeah, sure. Maybe, I frowned. Someday.

Karen Staedter

The Hem of His Garment—Mark 5:34
Your faith has made you whole...

The Hem of His Garment is a point of contact
Where one goes to reach out in faith
Believing in where the answer lies
And seeking to meet it face to face
The woman in the story in Mark chapter 5
Had a problem and could not find a cure
She heard about Jesus and knew who He was
She sought Him out just to be sure
Her faith in Jesus the Son of Man and of God
Never wavered as she pushed through the crowd
She simply knew He would be there for her
And at His feet she humbly bowed
Just as she had thought He was the answer
Immediately she was made whole
Her faith led her to the hem of His garment
Reaching down into the depths of her soul
Jesus has the power to save and to heal
We must be willing to seek Him out
We have to reach the point of contact
And approach it without any doubt
As a believer child of God
Great things you will be able to do
By faith put your faith in God and see
The hem of His garment can be you
God can make you the point of contact
Where others can reach out to and find Jesus Christ
Take His love and power to others freely
He has already paid the price
Become the hem of His garment
By sharing what He has given to you
Your faith has indeed made you whole
And it can prove to others God's word is true

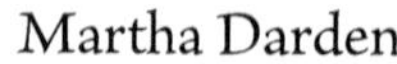

Martha Darden

Impacting Hope

The air is raw and chill;
I myself have witnessed the effects
An unpleasant feeling; yet I am too still
To trounce this terminal neglect
That leaves people with nil.
Our world turns with defects,
But we must extend ourselves to the hopeless.
For many, help is out of reach.
If we gather our unwavering minds,
We can lift them to their feet.
The patterns of this world could be re-defined.
Impact is within our grasp;
Will we hold it or release?
This is a question many pass.
If neglect is obsolete,
Nothing will restrain this world to its knees.

Claire Nichole Lennard

First Painter

Da Vinci and Van Gogh were not the first
To paint the beauties of the universe;
It was rather the One who made
The creation in which the stars were laid.
He had an infinite canvas
On which to paint the very best.
He held a brush yet used no smock,
For greens flew to grass and grays soared to rocks,
Blues found the oceans, and beige went to sand,
Colors countless designed for man.
A few cans of paint were spilled,
And so sunrise and sunset were filled,
In tawny gold and the brightest pinks,
Royal blue when the moon winks.
His strokes were clean and crisp
As He gave few clouds gentle wisps;
Flowers began like tiny rainbows,
Centerpieces lovely amidst all which grows
In colors galore and details plenty,
Diversity giving joy to many.
The Painter admires from overhead His toil,
More priceless than any other collection rare and royal.

Sarah Marie Williamson

We Are the Earth

We are the earth,
Wind and fire.
We are a speck and a dust.
We are time in eternity,
Bright stars in night
Shining forever.

We are the tears,
Yours and mine.
They run together
To make an ocean
In search of a desert
To sooth a thirst
Of a child and to bloom
Flowers in wilderness.

We are smiles,
Yours and mine
To make music to echo
Tallest mountains.

We are lovers,
To care for one another
To hold from falling
When the storms are too great.
And we hold peace together
Until we die.
Until we die.

Joy Lee

The Dreaded Wedding Bells

It started with the bells,
The dreaded wedding bells.
It began with a kiss,
The anticipated first kiss.
It ended with a death,
A sad, untimely death.
They stare at the ashes—
The ashes of today,
The ashes of the memories,
The memories of a wedding,
Of a wedding gone wrong.
The ashes show the sadness,
The ashes show the death.
She's thinking of the screams,
The shrill, chilling screams.
She's thinking of the bodies,
The poor, struggling bodies.
It was the end of all they know,
The end of all they loved.
They were burned with the fire,
The large, horrid fire.
It started with the bells,
The dreaded wedding bells.
It began with a kiss,
The anticipated first kiss.
It ended with the deaths,
The sad, untimely deaths.

Sam Nagel

Winter Walk

A lonely traveler on his long walk home throws his heavy army bag
over his shoulder and treads on through the snow.
The snow is deep, the pathway narrow.
There is no wind the sky is dark, except for the dancing Northern Lights.
The silence is frightening, the cold is biting.
Icicles hang from his eyelashes and hood of his parker.
His breath hangs like a hazy fog before him.
Each step he takes sounds like two wooden spoons being rubbed together.
Off in the distance he hears the forlorn sound of a lonely wolf
echo through the still night air.
From out of nowhere a choir of voices returns that forlorn howl.
He knows that pack of wolves isn't far away.
Too spite the cold and even colder shiver runs up and down his spine.
He quickens his pace and wraps his coat a little tighter around his body.
Snow begins to fall; the flakes are big like feather down.
The pines and spruce trees are dark against the snow.
A rabbit dares out on the path before him and hurries into the woods.
Then like a beacon in the night he spots the lights from the farmhouse
he grew up in.
Half running, half walking he hurries towards the house.
As he draws nearer he sees the smoke rising straight up into the night
sky from the farmhouse chimney. He hears the barking of his own dog
that was just a puppy when he went to war.
His hand grabs the doorknob and he flings open the door.
He is standing in the warm kitchen of his familiar home.
He tosses down his army bag, his golden lab barking and jumping up and
down on him. His mom and dad descend the stairs in their night clothes.
and are immediately at his side. Tears of joy fill the old folks' eyes as
they embrace their only son. The years have turned their hair silver and
time has shown their age.
But all at once in that brief moment it's as though he has never been away.
The deed is done—the son is home from war.

June Stanchell

Secret Vows

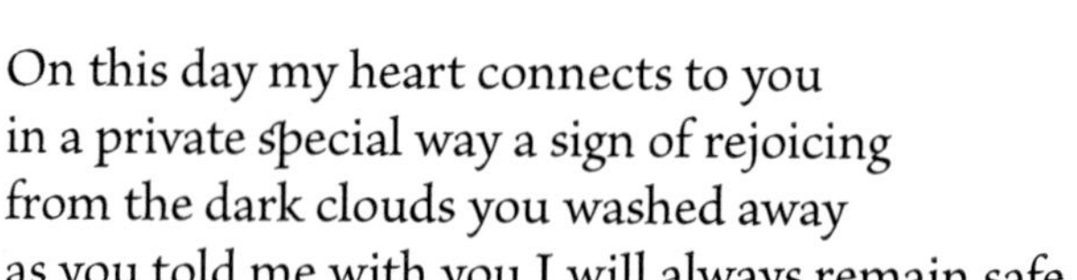

On this day my heart connects to you
in a private special way a sign of rejoicing
from the dark clouds you washed away
as you told me with you I will always remain safe.

Inside the cracks of my mind
is a feeling that is a one-of-a-kind reaction
knowing you are entirely all mine.

Two hearts now combine forever in our
lifetime as my eyes stare into yours.
Your love I will always adore
then return to you so much more.
These images are delicate and fine
as I now stand beside this husband of mine.

He now looks into my eyes
with care, and in delight then begins
to recite those special words to me.
Every line sets his love completely free
as the passion flows directly
settling and resting inside me.

As our lips touch so softly standing strong
with a glow that will constantly show.
Now the world finally knows they all rise to their toes
as the announcement has been made
look to the right I now stand as your wife.

For the rest of our lives we will remember this day
as we looked into each other's eyes and released
those words so heartfelt and pure the very sounds
with touching nouns are known to us as our
precious wedding secret vows.

Laura Wright

My love for poetry and spoken words go way back as far as my high school years. Writing to me is not just an outlet; it is an expression of who I really am underneath the very core of me. I am in another state of mind dreams when I write. It allows me to be free and travel inside the beautiful words I write. My grandma has been my biggest inspiration she believed in me from the first poem I wrote, and even though she has passed on now I still feel her inside me cheering me on. I feel her pat me on the back saying, "Good job, baby, Grandma loves you and believes in you." She always taught me that you can achieve your dreams if you believe in yourself and your potential.

Our Universe

Upon eyes bestowing vision, trust
not reflections without balance of
self, upon days end the mortal
body tattered and torn, without energy
yet the mind has only begun

Knowledge a state of being, life a
gift one must challenge to thrive
within mother's girth, elements spin round
and round touch the sky kissing earth

Balance the natural knowing self thrive
as one within our universe.

Timothy E. New

Forget Me

I gave so much to you
and you tore my heart in two.
I thought I could trust you,
now I'm trying to escape you.
You tore my heart apart,
now my love is lost,
and I'm trying to find the pieces in the fire of your heart.
You burnt up all my dreams and you crushed all my love,
now I'm staying away.
Now I'm staring at the walls of forgotten love.
I tried to make you change,
I tried to make you mine,
but you found out what I tried to do
and you found a place to hide.
You wanted some things
and I gave what I had
and you took my love for granted
and you left me all sad.
Now I'm forgetting you one memory at a time.
I wish you could see what you did to me.
At the time I did not realize you did not want me,
to make you mine.
Your soul is cold, you have no heart,
now I'm walking down the street of broken hearts.

Caitlyn Whitten

A Note for Girls

There are days
Where the pressure you feel
Is like a ton of bricks
That makes you lose your will.

Celebrities and models,
Size zero and thin,
It's in our society
The way it's always been.

As the pressure grows
Into an epidemic,
You may wrap yourself in thorns
And try to conform to be activistic.

Many girls
Feel that pressure.
You're not alone,
We'll make it together.

As someone once said
In her attempt to affect,
"Love is louder
Than the pressure to be perfect."

So try to stay strong
And believe in yourself.
You are unique
And there's nobody else.

Mikaela Danielle Brown

A Friend

I sometimes dream
Of having a friend,
One that will be there
Until the end.

A friend that is there
When I need a hand,
One that will be there
Until the end.

Someone I can count on,
On whom I can depend.
One that will be there
Until the end.

My friend is here.
My friend is near.
The one that will be there
Until the end.

Now I dream
That you'll have a friend,
One that will be there
Until the end.

Deekota Polk

Love Flows

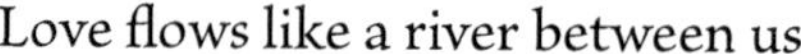

Love flows like a river between us

I don't wonder what heaven is like.
I have found it here on earth.
Since I found you and the love that
flows between us.

We dance the dance of love,
fitting together like matching gloves.
Moving to the rhythm of love
as it flows.

I long for the time we will always be
side by side
together so we can share our lives on
a daily basis, sharing the joy of our passion
and feeling the storms of emotions between us.

I opened my heart to you and let you in
and found a love so strong that flows
freely between us.
I dreamt of such a love never thinking I would
be so lucky as to find it.

Even though we spend many weeks and months
apart our love grows.
You are always in my heart and on my mind.

I love you with all my heart and soul, and wait patiently
for your return when you are gone,
waiting to build a special life together never more to be apart.
I love you, honey, hurry home.

Cecelia Anne Smith Cameron

I raised my children myself and have worked all my life. Still do to help my son when he needs me to. Writing has been a passion as long as I can remember. I write from my heart most of the time. This poem is for my love who is gone overseas for months at a time.

Golden Dawn and Black Midnight

The sun rises over the sea
The moon shines through the tree.
The day lets go of the gold
And the night has the black to hold
The sky has flecks of bright white
While pink cloud float over the sunset as a sight
I play my music when sitting on a stump
Flipping through songs, the sun looks like a bump
The rolling hills of green and yellow
Sit on the horizon by the sun, calm and mellow
I stand on the porch, silently leaning
Watching the orb rise, white and beaming
A bird sweeps down in the park for a bite
The golden view vanishes into the lines of earth
The black sky and white sphere fade into the golden birth
The sun always rises over the sea
And the moon will follow, shining brightly through the tree

Alina Brown-Smith

Index

CPSIA information can be obtained at www.ICGtesting.com
Printed in the USA
BVOW021837080712

294585BV00003B/1/P